Editor

Patricia Bahree M.A.

Editorial Assistants

Jacqueline Joyce
Gloria Renner-Thomas

Managing Editor

Eric B. Inglefield B.A.

Production

Keith Ireland
Eva Wrennall
Penny Kitchenham

© Macdonald & Co Ltd 1974
This edition published in 1987 by Black Cat, an
imprint of Macdonald & Co (Publishers) Ltd,
Greater London House, Hampstead Road,
London NW1.

Printed in Great Britain
ISBN 0-7481-0033-4

DISCOVERING THE ANCIENT PAST

DISCOVERING THE ANCIENT PAST

Michael Gibson

BLACK CAT

CONTENTS

DISCOVERING THE ANCIENT PAST

An Egyptian queen is enjoying a banquet. Around her, people are eating and talking while musicians play sweet music on their pipes. This all happened thousands of years ago. The palace that once rang with their laughter is now a heap of ruins baking in the sun.

How do we know about this queen and all the millions of people who lived before us? This is the work of archaeologists and historians. Archaeologists study the ruins and objects that ancient peoples left behind them. Historians read what these people wrote long ago.

This book tells you some of the things that archaeologists and historians have discovered about the peoples of the ancient past. As you read you will see that although these peoples lived long ago they were not very different from ourselves.

DIGGING UP THE PAST

Have you ever seen an Egyptian mummy? You can see one in a museum. You can also see golden daggers and beautiful jewellery worn thousands of years ago. Most of these things have been found by archaeologists.

Archaeologists dig up and study the things left behind by people who lived long ago. Lots of other people help them. Botanists help them study the remains of plants. Zoologists help them study ancient bones. People who have learned ancient languages help them read messages written long ago.

Plantain pollen

Oak pollen

Chrysanthemum pollen

Archaeologists find pollen grains. These tell what kind of plants grew long ago

Finding a site

At first archaeology was mainly a treasure hunt. Archaeologists set out to find lost palaces and the tombs of kings. Archaeologists are still interested in these things. But they also want to know what people wore and ate and how they lived.

To find out, archaeologists try to locate the sites of ancient towns or villages. When they have found a likely place, the dig begins.

At a dig

Most of the things people used thousands of years ago have been slowly buried under layers of earth. To find them, archaeologists dig a number of pits in the ground. They leave thick walls of earth called balks in between the pits. Each pit is carefully numbered and marked on a map.

Many things archaeologists have dug up are kept in museums. These paintings, statues and daggers are from Egypt

Can you see the different layers of earth in the pits? They are marked by labels

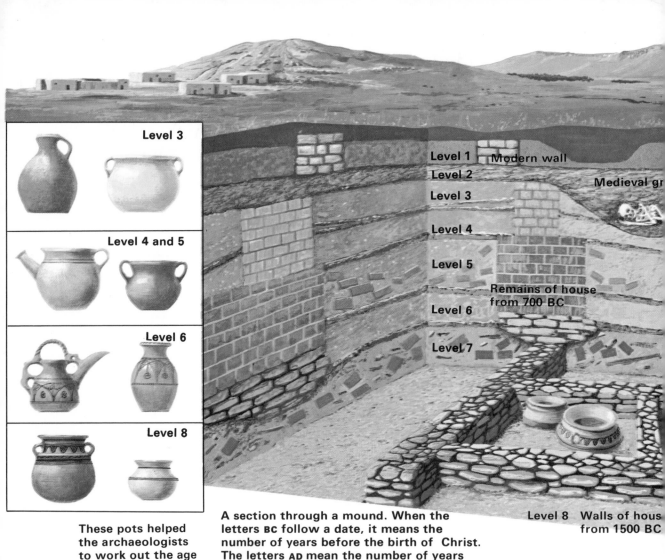

Level 3

Level 4 and 5

Level 6

Level 8

Level 1 Modern wall
Level 2
Level 3
Medieval gr
Level 4
Level 5
Remains of house
from 700 BC
Level 6
Level 7
Level 8 Walls of hous
from 1500 BC

These pots helped
the archaeologists
to work out the age
of each layer

A section through a mound. When the
letters BC follow a date, it means the
number of years before the birth of Christ.
The letters AD mean the number of years
after the birth of Christ.

The layers of earth

The oldest layer of earth is at the bottom of a pit. The newest is
at the top. These layers help archaeologists to work out how
old the things they find are. These layers of earth are called
strata. One layer is called a stratum. There are eight strata in
the dig below.

Archaeologists find different kinds of pots in the different
layers. These pots tell archaeologists a lot about the people who
lived on the site. Ancient peoples usually made the same kind
of pot for a very long time. So if archaeologists find a new type
of pot on the site, it usually means that a new people had
taken over.

14

The bones archaeologists find on a site can help them discover when people lived there

Dating the past

The remains of people and houses are often dated by the designs of pots and tools found nearby. Sometimes the Carbon 14 test is used. All living things contain a kind of carbon called Carbon 14. When they die, the Carbon 14 gradually disappears. Scientists can tell how old a piece of wood or bone is by measuring how much Carbon 14 is left.

Bones can also be dated by the Fluorine test. Old bones gradually absorb a chemical called fluorine from the soil. By measuring the amount of fluorine in a bone, archaeologists can tell how old it is.

A third way is the tree ring method. Every year a tree adds another ring to its size.

Measuring fluorine in bones

When archaeologists find an old house containing timbers cut from tree trunks, they can compare rings in the timber wood with rings in living local trees. This often tells them when the house was built.

Tree rings are thicker in wet years than in dry ones. The logs in old houses can be compared with living local trees to find out when a house was built

A hot, dry summer

A warm, wet summer

In the Southern United States archaeologists have traced the patterns of tree rings back hundreds of years

15

An archaeologist must work carefully when he finds something

Archaeologists use tools such as picks and trowels

Finds must be cleaned and photographed. Their position is plotted on a map

Digging

At a site, the archaeologists remove the top soil with picks and shovels. When an archaeologist thinks he is getting near something important, he works with a tiny trowel and a brush. He has to be careful not to break anything lying in the soil. When he finds something, he brushes the earth off it carefully.

Measuring

The next thing he has to do is to measure the exact position of his find. He gets a tape measure and measures from the object to two of the wooden pegs around the pit. Then, he marks the object's place on a map of the site.

Now he needs to know how far below the ground the object is. He measures carefully and notes the depth in his records. Often, the archaeologist takes a photograph of his find before removing it. Finally, the object is put in a bag marked with a label saying exactly where it was found.

Is this a site or an ordinary piece of land? It is hard to tell. From the air, archaeologists can see that it is a buried city

Archaeology from the air

Can you guess why archaeologists use aeroplanes? They use them to find sites that cannot be seen from the ground. Sometimes photographs taken from the air show the ruins of ancient buildings. Often the plants in a field show the outlines of old walls and ditches.

Can you see the old walls and ditches?

When plants grow on top of buried walls, they have less soil to grow in. They get less water than the rest of the plants in the field, so they are smaller and lighter in colour than the other plants. When plants grow on top of an ancient ditch, they are usually bigger and darker in colour than the other plants. This is because the ditch contains rich soil which the plants feed on.

17

Divers lifting wine jars out of the wreck of a Roman ship

Underwater archaeology

Underwater archaeology can be very exciting. Sometimes underwater archaeologists find whole towns that disappeared under the sea long ago. This may have happened when there was a terrible earthquake. It may have been caused by the ocean flooding the land.

Many shipwrecks lie on the ocean floor. The famous diver Jacques Cousteau and his crew have explored many wrecks. Once, they found a Roman ship with hundreds of wine jars in it.

After the dig

Digging things up is only the beginning for the archaeologist. Next, he makes sure that the things he has found do not crumble into dust by treating them with chemicals.

How ancient pots were used

The archaeologist asks scientists to carry out tests on the bones, bits of wood and pieces of leather he has found. These tests tell him how long ago the people who built the town lived.

When this has been done, the archaeologist thinks hard about what he has found. He asks himself many questions. How did the people get their food? What kind of houses did they have? What kind of religion did they believe in? Gradually, he writes a complete description of how they lived.

Then he compares his finds with what other archaeologists have found in other places. Were his people the same as those who lived nearby or were they different?

We can put together a picture of life long ago thanks to the work of archaeologists

19

STONE AGE PEOPLE

We do not know for sure when the first people appeared on Earth. For millions of years there were animals similar to present day apes. These animals were probably the ancestors of both men and the modern apes. Over millions of years, they slowly changed. Archaeologists have discovered the bones of some of these man-like creatures.

The Southern Apes

Bones of the Southern Apes have been found in several places in Africa. The Southern Apes walked upright on their hind legs. Their brains were bigger than those of modern apes, but only about half the size of ours.

Pithecanthropus

Pithecanthropus means ape-like man. These ape-men had larger brains and were bigger and stronger than the Southern Apes. They used stone tools and made fires.

Southern Ape

The Neanderthals were good hunters. They buried their dead and may have been the first people to have a religion

The Neanderthals

Later still, the Neanderthals appeared. They are named after the Neander Valley in Germany where their bones were first discovered. They had much bigger brains than the ape-men. Their brains were even larger than ours. They made good stone tools.

Cro-Magnon man

Finally, our closest ancestors appeared. They were called Cro-Magnon men because their bones were first discovered at Cro-Magnon in southern France. Although their brains were slightly smaller than the Neanderthals, they seem to have been more intelligent.

Neanderthal Man   Cro-Magnon Man

Some Cro-Magnon people lived in caves and made fine clothes out of animal skins

The Piltdown skull. The bones had been dyed to make them look old and the teeth had been filed down to mislead the scientists. In 1953 tests finally proved that the bones were not really those of a strange ape-man

The man who never was

Have you ever heard of Piltdown man?

Around 1900, some unusual bones were found near the town of Piltdown in England. When scientists put them together, they formed an odd creature with a man's skull and an ape's jaw. Many scientists thought he was the missing link between men and apes.

In 1953, tests were done on the skull. The results showed that the bones had been stained to make them look old. They were really those of a fairly modern man and a young orang-utan.

Piltdown man taught the scientists a lesson. Now they test everything very carefully. They do not want to be tricked by another man who never was.

The head bones were those of a fairly modern man

The jaw bones were those of a young orang-utan

Hunting and Gathering

The first people lived by hunting and gathering. They picked fruits from the trees and bushes and pulled up plants to eat their roots. They killed small animals and stole birds' eggs.

Old Stone Age hunters

The Old Stone Age is the period of time when people first started making stone weapons and tools.

When Stone Age men wanted to catch a large animal, they made a trap. They dug a deep pit in the ground and stuck sharp sticks in the bottom. They covered the hole with sticks and leaves.

Stone Age hunters dug pits to catch large animals. Stakes were driven into the sides of the pits

If a large animal walked onto the twigs, it fell through onto the sharp sticks below. Then, the hunters rushed over to the hole and threw rocks and spears at the animal to kill it.

Dogs were the first animals that Stone Age people tamed

The bow and arrow

Towards the end of the Old Stone Age, men invented the bow and arrow. The bow was a marvellous invention. Its arrows raced through the air so fast that hunters could kill an animal before the animal knew it was in danger. Hunters made several types of arrows. Some had sharp flint heads.

A sabre-toothed tiger falls into a pit

Middle Stone Age hunters

About 12,000 BC, people started to make much better weapons and tools. This period is called the Middle Stone Age.

Man's best friend

Middle Stone Age people made friends with dogs. Dogs hung round their camps hoping for scraps of food. Gradually, they became tame. Men were able to teach them to drive wild animals into traps. This is how the dog became man's best friend.

Making Tools, Clothes and Houses

Stone tools

About a million and a half years ago, ape-men started to make simple stone tools. At first they broke pebbles into two and used the sharp edges as knives. Later, they discovered that a rock called flint broke quite easily into sharp pieces. They hit a lump of flint with a stone until it broke.

Later still, they found that they could make the edge of the flint much sharper by breaking off tiny pieces. They did this by pressing the edge of the tool with a piece of wood. This is called pressure flaking.

By about 7000 BC, people had learned to make very beautiful and useful stone tools.

Tools were made by hitting stones together until they broke

Late Stone Age people made fine tools from flint. Flint axes were fitted into wooden handles

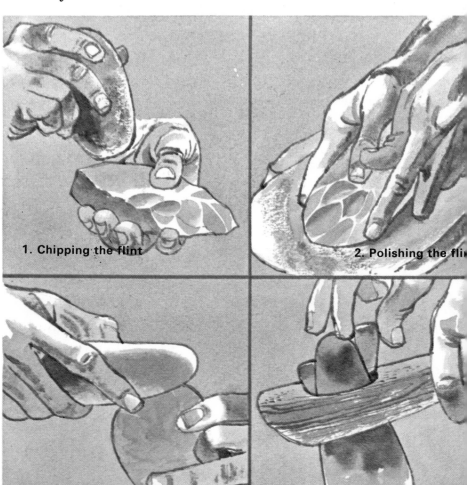

1. Chipping the flint

2. Polishing the fli

3. Sharpening the edge

4. Putting on a hand

A flint mine

Flint mines

To get flint to make tools, Stone Age people dug mines in the
ground. Archaeologists have found several flint mines. One is
at Grimes Graves in England. The tool makers dug great pits
with spades made of animals' shoulder blades. They chopped
lumps of flint from the walls with picks made of reindeer antlers.

Flint was not the only thing tools were made of. Bones were
made into spades and spearheads as well as needles and
harpoons. Lots of tools were made of wood but these have rotted
away.

Scraping

Cutting

Sewing

Making clothes from skins

The earliest people did not
wear any clothes at all. They
may have been covered in
thick hair and so did not need any.

Making clothes

Then, the weather got colder and much of
Europe, Asia, and North America was covered
in ice for thousands of years. This period is
called the Ice Age. People must have worn
clothes to protect themselves against the bitter
cold. None of these clothes have survived. But
archaeologists have found lots of needles which
were probably used to make clothes. A few cave
paintings show men, who may have been
priests, wearing animal skins.

The picture above shows how we think early
men and women made their clothes. After
killing wild animals, they cut off their skins.
They scraped off all the fat with a flint tool and
stretched the skin in the sun to dry. They cut
the skins and sewed the pieces together with
bone needles and leather thread.

**Archaeologists
have found bone
needles like these**

Spinning

After taming sheep, people learned to cut off their wool and make cloth. They twisted pieces of wool together to make strong threads. Sometimes they used stones called spindle whorls to weigh down the thread and make spinning easier.

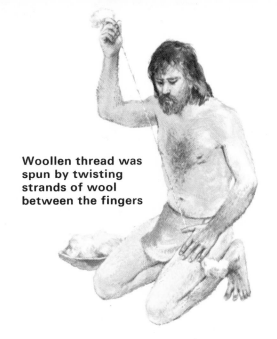

Woollen thread was spun by twisting strands of wool between the fingers

Woollen thread was woven into cloth

Weaving

They fixed a number of threads to a wooden frame called a loom. It seems the first looms were upright. Stone balls were tied onto the bottom of the threads to keep them taut. These stone balls have been found on many New Stone Age sites.

The up and down threads are called the warp. Another thread called the weft was passed in and out of the warp. In this way, people were able to weave cloth.

Once the cloth was finished, it was dipped in bowls of dye made from vegetable juices, roots and coloured earths. When the cloth was dry, it could be cut up and made into clothes.

29

Building houses

The first people did not have houses. They must have slept on the ground or in trees.

An early tent made from animal skins

Some early people lived in caves. Caves made nice safe homes, but there cannot have been enough of them to go around. Many families must have scooped out shallow holes in the ground and covered them with branches and leaves.

Later, people lived in tents made of animal skins. The first villages were not built until about 10,000 BC. At Jericho, one of the world's earliest towns, the people built round houses. The walls were made of sun-dried brick. The roofs were made of branches covered with mud. The floors, which were lower than the ground outside, were made of beaten clay. Some of the houses only had one room. Others had as many as three.

A Swiss village built on wooden piles

One of the houses in the ancient settlement at Skara Brae. Can you guess how each piece of stone furniture was used?

Lake Villages

In about 2000 BC, people living in Switzerland built several hundred lake villages. Thick wooden posts were stuck into the bed of a lake. Then, wooden platforms were built with houses on top of them. Lots of things fell into the lake and sank into the mud. Archaeologists have dug up these things.

Houses of stone

The most amazing prehistoric homes of all are at Skara Brae in the Orkney Islands, Scotland. All the houses were joined together like an anthill. They were all made of stone. Even the furniture was made of stone. The roofs were made of skins stretched across whale bones. There was a hole in each roof to let the light in and the smoke out.

Many early houses had stone walls and thatched roofs

The inside of the house was simple

31

A bison painted by Stone Age people on the wall of the Lascaux caves

Cave Paintings

Finding the paintings at Lascaux

One day in 1940, four boys and their dog went for a walk on the hills at Lascaux in France. Suddenly, the dog disappeared. Soon, the boys heard him howling. Where could he be? At last, they found him. He had tumbled into a hole close to a fallen tree.

One of the boys jumped into the hole. As he picked the dog up, he noticed a tunnel leading down into the earth.

The next morning, the boys returned with a lamp and made their way down the tunnel into a long cave. When they looked at the walls, they saw marvellous paintings of huge bulls, deer and many other animals.

The boys rushed home and told their teacher. He went back with them. What he saw made him very excited. He sent for the most famous archaeologist in France. The archaeologist said that the paintings had been made by Stone Age people and were the finest cave paintings he had ever seen.

Lamp · Paints · Fur pad · Twig · Feather · Blow pipe

Tools for painting

Priests may have danced and carried out magical rites in front of the paintings ▶

Painting the caves

The Stone Age artists made their paints from vegetables, fruits and different coloured earths mixed with animal fat. Sometimes they rubbed animal fat on the cave wall and blew dry paint on it.

A few paintings of people have been found. Most are of animals. Many of the animals seem to have arrows sticking in them. The cave people probably believed that the paintings were magical. They thought that they would help them to kill large numbers of animals.

Painting animals on a cave wall

The First Farmers

Throughout most of the Stone Age, people lived by hunting and gathering. It was not until about 8000 BC that people first learned to grow crops and raise animals. The first farmers lived in the lands around modern-day Israel, Jordan, Iraq and southern Russia.

Why did farming start in this part of the world? Because wild wheat and barley grew in this area. Someone must have discovered that seeds could be planted and crops grown.

Dogs had already been tamed. This must have encouraged people to try to tame the wild sheep, pigs and cattle that lived nearby.

Once people started farming, they changed their whole way of life. Instead of following the herds of wild animals, they were able to settle down and build villages.

A New Stone Age village

New Stone Age people invented pot making

They decorated their pots with lines made with their finger nails or pieces of wood

34

A time of changes

The first farmers are called the New Stone Age people. They still made stone tools but they had learned to weave cloth and make houses of mud bricks. The beginning of farming and the many other changes in the way people lived is called the New Stone Age Revolution.

Pots were baked in an oven or kiln to make them hard

Making pots

One of the most useful discoveries made by New Stone Age people was how to make clay pots. Some people probably found that they could make shapes with wet clay. Soon, they started to make pots by the coil method. They rolled clay into long sausages and wound them round and round. When the pots were finished, they were baked to make them hard.

1. The top of the pot was made and dried

2. Then the bottom half was added

3. The hole in the bottom was closed

4. The pot was baked

Slash and burn farmers

The earliest farmers cut down trees and burnt them and grew crops in the wood ashes. This is called slash and burn farming. They farmed the same fields until they had used up all the goodness in the soil. Then they moved to new land.

Farmers left their homes in the Middle East because they needed new land to farm. They made their way to Egypt and other places near the Mediterranean Sea. They took their tamed animals with them. People in the lands they moved to copied them and learned how to raise animals and crops.

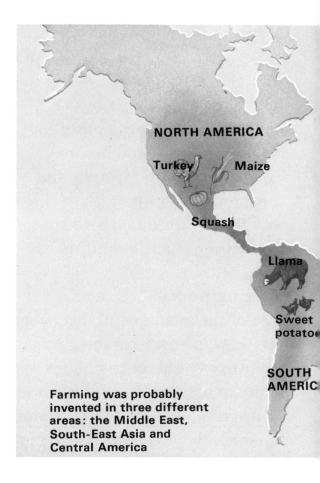

Farming was probably invented in three different areas: the Middle East, South-East Asia and Central America

Early farmers cleared the land by cutting down trees and burning them

Farmers on the move

One group of farmers moved westwards across Europe. They are called the Danubian people. They reached Germany in about 3000 BC. The first farmers to reach Britain arrived in about 4000 BC. They are called the Windmill Hill people.

Another group of people were moving eastwards across Iran towards Asia. They reached India in about 3500 BC and northern China much later.

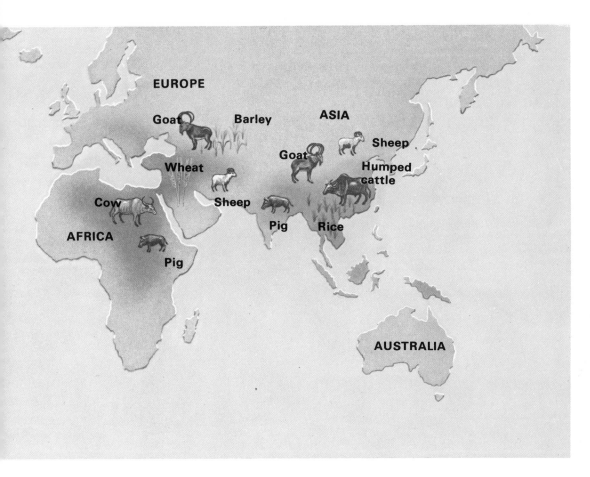

Three different beginnings?

In South-East Asia, people grew rice instead of wheat and barley. Their cows, pigs and sheep were quite different from those in the Middle East. This may be because they had their own separate New Stone Age Revolution.

By about 3000 BC, farmers in Mexico grew maize, squashes and sweet potatoes. They had no cows or sheep at all. Was the idea of farming brought to America by people who sailed across the oceans? Or did America have its own Revolution?

At the present moment, it seems farming was invented in three different places at about the same time.

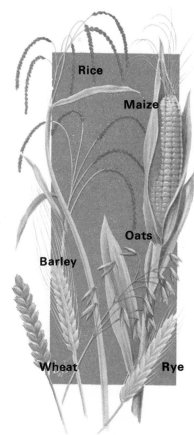

Can you find these people in the picture above?

THE SUMERIANS

The picture above was made thousands of years ago. The people who made it were called the Sumerians. The top of the picture shows a Sumerian king meeting with his court. At the bottom, fish, rams and bullocks are being brought as gifts for the king.

The Sumerians lived in a part of the world called Mesopotamia. They were short dark-haired people. Some men wore sheepskin skirts with the wool on the outside. Other men and women dressed in garments made of cloth. Like the men in the picture, many Sumerians shaved their heads. Other men had beards and long hair.

The land between the rivers

Mesopotamia means 'the land between the rivers'. The rivers that run through Mesopotamia are the Tigris and Euphrates. Can you find them on the map?

Year after year these rivers carried tonnes of fine earth down to the coast. New land built up where the rivers met the sea. This land is called the delta.

The Sumerians settled in the delta lands around 5000 BC. The rivers often flooded leaving behind rich soil that was good for growing crops.

Slowly, the Sumerians built the first great civilization. They were the first people to build cities, the first to use the wheel, the first to write and the first to work out a calendar.

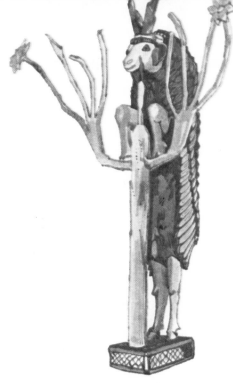

The Sumerians were the first people to make beautiful statues such as this one out of bronze

The main cities of Mesopotamia are shown on the map

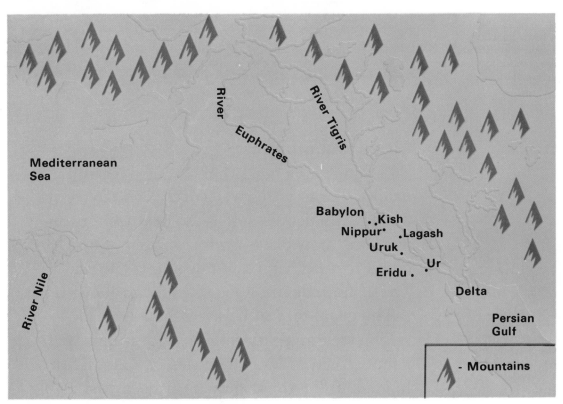

Cities and Kings

Sumerian cities were surrounded by brick walls. At the centre of the city was a high building called a ziggurat.

The Sumerians believed that each city was ruled by a different god. The god was supposed to live in a temple on top of the ziggurat.

A high building called a ziggurat towered above most Sumerian cities

Ziggurats rose up like a wedding cake in a series of tiers. A temple was built at the top

Cities and mounds

The Sumerians built their cities with sun-dried bricks. These cities were often destroyed by floods. The people smoothed down the ruins and built new cities on top of them. Soon the cities rose on high mounds above the plain. These mounds are good sites for archaeologists.

The great city of Ur stretched several kilometres in all directions. Thousands of people lived in Ur. The cities of Kish, Eridu, Lagash and Nippur may have been just as big.

Ruling the cities

Each Sumerian city was the centre of a small state. The city and state were ruled by a king. The king collected taxes, led the army and made sure the city ran smoothly.

The king and queen lived in an enormous palace. They had many servants. In the evening, the king met his nobles in a grand hall. Music was played for them on flutes and harps. Jars of beer stood on the floor. The guests drank it through long metal straws.

A king giving orders to his general

The musicians are playing several instruments. What modern instruments do they remind you of?

41

The royal graves of Ur

In 1928, an archaeologist called Leonard Woolley discovered what may be the graves of the kings and queens of the city of Ur. One of the men buried in the graves was called A-bar-gi. When he died his body was dressed in rich clothes. It was carried to a deep, wide pit and laid on a platform. Weapons and tools were laid beside it.

Later, a crowd of people walked down a slope into the grave. They were probably nobles, officials, soldiers and servants.

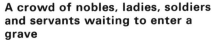
A crowd of nobles, ladies, soldiers and servants waiting to enter a grave

The women in the grave wore wigs and beautiful golden headdresses

Doomed to die

The ladies were dressed in splendid clothes.
They wore huge wigs decorated with lovely
jewellery made of gold.

Oxen pulled two finely carved and painted
carts into the grave. Servants arrived with a
jar of wine and cups. Beautiful music was
played on a harp. It seemed like a party, but it
was not. Poison had been added to the wine.
All of the people drank the wine and died. The
oxen were killed. Then the grave was filled in.

Leonard Woolley found the bodies of sixty-
two people in A-bar-gi's grave. Close by, he
found twenty-five people buried in the grave of
a woman named Shub-ad who may have been
a queen.

Some of the
jewellery Leonard
Woolley found. It
is now in a museum

Rich Sumerians handing gifts for the gods to a priest

Gods and Priests

The Sumerians gave their gods many presents. They thought that goats, jugs of milk, and bags of grain would make them happy. They also gave them small statues. These had wide eyes and their hands were clasped in front of them. The Sumerians believed that these statues would pray to the gods for them.

The Sumerians thought that each city was ruled by the god who lived on top of the ziggurat. There were many other gods as well. Enlil was the god of the air and Anu the god of the sky. Rabiscu was an evil spirit who lurked in dark corners.

Priest-kings

The Sumerians believed that the gods were all powerful and that they would be punished if they angered the gods. The first kings were probably high priests. They were thought to rule the city according to the wishes of the gods.

A long Sumerian poem tells the story of one such priest-king. He was called Gilgamesh and ruled the city of Uruk. He tried to find a way to live forever. In the end, he found that he had to die like every other person.

Priests sacrificed animals to the gods

The Sumerian temples had their own lands where the priests worked

Temple work

The Sumerians believed that their gods were alive. The priests fed their statues, clothed them and made sure they had every luxury possible.

The priests had many other jobs. They led the religious rites and the celebrations on holidays. Those who knew how to read and write kept records for the city. The temple owned a lot of land which the priests farmed. They also took care of temple cattle.

45

The farmers are cutting ditches down to the river. When they open the gate, the river will flow into the ditches and water the fields

Growing Crops

We know about the Sumerians mainly through the ruins of their great cities. The cities depended on the farmers in the countryside. These farmers ploughed the land and irrigated it with canals bringing water from the rivers. The farmers grew more food than they needed so that they could sell food to the people in the cities.

At first the Sumerians used barley as money

Oxen pulled wooden ploughs

Ways of farming

The Sumerians were clever farmers and their ways of doing things are still used in some places. They ploughed the land with wooden ploughs and harvested their crops with sickles.

They separated the chaff from the grain by throwing them up in the air. The wind blew the chaff away. The heavy grain fell straight down.

The Sumerians ground the grain between two pieces of stone and used the flour to make meal. The Sumerians' main crop was barley. They also grew wheat and many vegetables.

The grain and chaff were separated. Then the grain was ground into flour

Words in Clay

This is an example of the oldest Sumerian writing. It is called pictographic writing because many of the signs are small pictures

This is cuneiform writing. Cuneiform characters were made with a reed pen which was shaped like a 'v' at the end

Writing cuneiform letters

The Sumerians invented writing. They began by drawing pictures on clay tablets. Later they used signs to stand for sounds. They made these signs with a reed pen shaped like a 'v' at the end. When pressed in the clay, it made a wedge-shaped mark. This kind of writing is called cuneiform writing.

The seal was rolled across a piece of clay leaving a clear impression behind

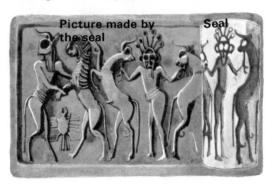

Picture made by the seal

Seal

Seals for signature
The Sumerians made stone seals. When rolled across wet clay, the seals left a picture of a carving. These pictures were like signatures. Everyone had his own seal.

Numbers and the calendar

The Sumerians used the numbers shown in the picture. These were also made with a wedge-shaped stylus. They worked out a calendar with 30 days in every month and 360 days in a year. This was not quite right so the priests sometimes added a month.

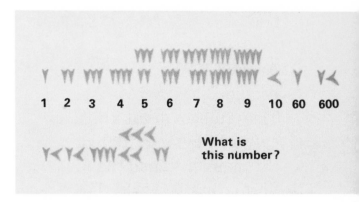

| 1 | 2 | 3 | 4 | 5 | 6 | 7 | 8 | 9 | 10 | 60 | 600 |

What is this number?

Cuneiform numbers

Reading the tablets

Experts today can read cuneiform writing. They think that the Sumerians invented writing so that they could keep records. The oldest tablets are lists of gifts given to the temple or goods traded by merchants. Later, writing was used for many other things. Some of the tablets are business letters and a few are stories and love songs.

Sumerian merchants kept lists of the things they bought and sold. These were written down by the scribes

Babylonians and Assyrians

Around 1700 BC a new group of people conquered Mesopotamia. They ruled a great kingdom called Babylonia. Babylon, the main city, had the first library in the world. The Babylonians copied the cuneiform script of the Sumerians. The library contained hundreds of clay tablets.

One of the most famous kings of Babylon was Hammurabi. He wrote a book of laws and had it carved in stone. There were 282 laws in all. One law said that if a man broke another's arm, his arm should be broken. A second law said that if a house fell down and killed the owner, the man who built the house should be killed.

The Babylonians were conquered by the Assyrians, but the city of Babylon remained great. The Assyrian king, Nebuchadnezzar, had the Hanging Gardens of Babylon built for his beautiful wife. The high walls and fabulous buildings of Babylon became famous throughout the world.

The beautiful Ishtar Gate was the main entrance to Babylon

Hunters and hounds from a scene carved by Assyrian artists

The Assyrians used huge siege engines and rams to knock down the walls and gates of cities. Their enemies tried to set these weapons on fire

The warrior kings

The Assyrians were famous for their well-trained armies. The king often rode at the head of his foot soldiers, charioteers, horse cavalry and camel troops.

People trembled when they heard the Assyrians were coming. It was said that they cut off the limbs of their enemies to steal their rings and bracelets. They also hung the skins of their enemies on their palace walls. The Assyrians boasted about their cruelty so no one would dare to disobey them.

When the Assyrian kings were not fighting, they were often hunting. They hunted lions from chariots with bows and arrows. Scenes of kings killing fierce lions were carved on their palace walls.

THE EGYPTIANS

The Life-Giving River

The Egyptians fished and hunted from boats made of reeds

The first great cities in Egypt grew up along the River Nile. The River Nile was important to the Egyptians. Every year the Nile overflowed its banks and spread thick, rich mud over the land. Plants grew well in this mud.

Many animals lived in the tall grasses along the Nile. The early Egyptians hunted wild sheep, gazelles and antelope. Lions and leopards prowled through the long grass looking for food. Hippopotami wallowed in the marshes. The Egyptians made boats from the reeds that grew along the Nile. They caught fish and hunted birds that lived among the reeds.

King Menes beats down his enemy with a club on this clay plaque

54

Two kingdoms

For many years there were two kingdoms in Egypt. One kingdom, Lower Egypt, grew up on the Nile delta. The delta was made of mud dropped by the Nile where it flows into the Mediterranean Sea. The second kingdom, Upper Egypt, was in the valley to the south.

In about 3200 BC, a ruler of Upper Egypt called Menes conquered Lower Egypt. He became the pharaoh or ruler of all Egypt. His crown was made up of the white crown of Upper Egypt and the red one of Lower Egypt.

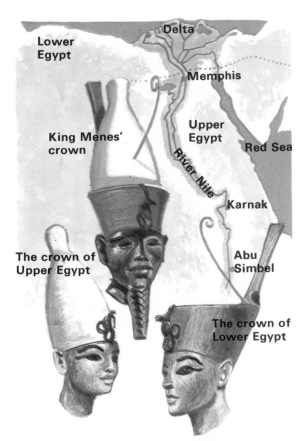

King Menes conquered all of Egypt and made the two crowns into one

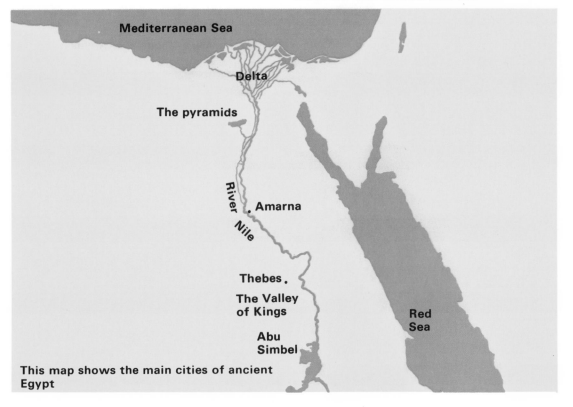

This map shows the main cities of ancient Egypt

A rich Egyptian watches his labourers gathering in the harvest

Food and farming

The River Nile flooded every summer. When the waters went down, the Egyptians planted their crops. Their main crops were wheat and barley, but they also grew onions, beans, radishes, carrots, cucumbers, grapes, melons and pomegranates.

THE FARMING YEAR

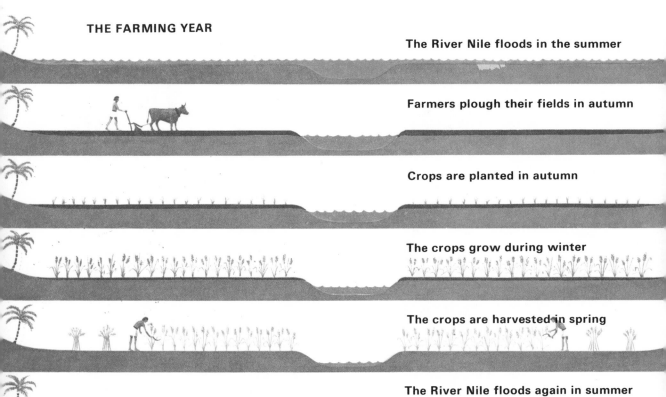

The River Nile floods in the summer

Farmers plough their fields in autumn

Crops are planted in autumn

The crops grow during winter

The crops are harvested in spring

The River Nile floods again in summer

Irrigation

Between March and June there was no rain at all. The farmers had to get water from the River Nile or their crops would die. They dug canals from the river to their fields. Then they lifted some of the water onto their fields with machines called shadoofs. The shadoof had a bucket made of leather on one end and a stone weight on the other.

Using a shadoof

Pigs treading the seed into newly ploughed fields

Sowing crops

Many Egyptian paintings show farming scenes. One shows farmers usings pigs to help them plant their crops. The pigs trod on the seeds and pushed them into the soil.

Making wine

The Egyptians used the grapes they grew to make wine. They squeezed the juice from the grapes with their bare feet. They stored the wine in jars. Egyptians drank a lot of wine and beer with meals of roast duck, vegetables, bread and cakes.

Wine making

57

Gods and Goddesses

The goddess Isis and the god Osiris

The jackal-headed god Anubis weighing a dead pharaoh's heart against the feather of truth

Horus

The Egyptians believed that when they died their bodies and souls parted. They thought that their souls went on a long journey. At the end of it, they were judged by the god Osiris. He put their heart on one side of a scale and the feather of truth on the other. If the scale tipped the wrong way, they were thrown to a frightful monster. If the scale showed they had been good, they entered heaven.

One of the most powerful gods was Amun-ra, the sun god. Some people believed that the pharaoh was the son of Amun-ra.

Other Egyptians believed the pharaoh was Horus, the son of the god Osiris. Osiris was supposed to have been an early pharaoh who taught the Egyptians to farm and build cities. He became so powerful that his brother Set grew jealous and murdered him. When his son Horus grew up, he defeated Set and brought his father back to life. Thus, many Egyptians believed that every pharaoh was Horus. When a pharaoh died, he became Osiris and his son became the new Horus.

Bast

Sekhmet

The Egyptians believed in many other gods. Some of them took the shape of animals.

Bast
Bast was the cat goddess. She loved music and dancing. The Egyptians thought that all cats were sacred. When cats died, they were mummified in honour of Bast.

Apis
Apis was the bull god. A sacred bull was kept in a temple to Apis at Memphis. The priests studied its every movement because they thought this would tell them what would happen in the future. When the bull died, it was mummified and buried in a magnificent tomb.

Isis

Amun-ra

Selket
Selket was a goddess who protected the dead. Her picture was often drawn inside mummy cases.

Sekmet
The goddess Sekmet had the head of a lion. She was the goddess of war.

Selket

Apis

Building a pyramid

The Pyramids and Mummies

The pharaohs wanted to be buried in tombs that would last for ever, so they built the pyramids. One of the finest is the Great Pyramid of Cheops.

The Great Pyramid is made of over two million blocks of stone. The biggest block weighs about fifteen tonnes and the ordinary ones about two and a half tonnes each.

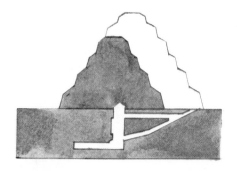

The first pyramid was built for the pharaoh Zoser. It is called a step pyramid because its sides look like huge steps

Building the pyramids

How did the Egyptians build the pyramids? They did not have any cranes to lift the heavy stones. We think that great long lines of slaves pushed and pulled the stones on wooden sledges up long ramps made of earth.

60

Inside a pyramid

Most pyramids had entrances on the north side. In the Great Pyramid of Cheops a passage led from the entrance to the Grand Gallery. The Grand Gallery led to the King's Chamber. This was where the pharaoh was buried with all his treasures.

After the pharaoh had been buried, the door to the King's Chamber was blocked with three huge blocks of stone. The corridor was filled with stones and the entrance was cunningly hidden. But tomb robbers still got in. They stole the King's riches long ago. Other passages in the pyramid led to empty chambers. These may have been built to confuse tomb robbers.

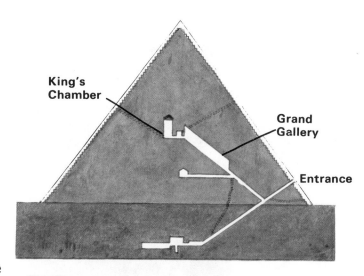

King's Chamber

Grand Gallery

Entrance

The Great Pyramid of Cheops. The Pharaoh was buried in the King's Chamber

61

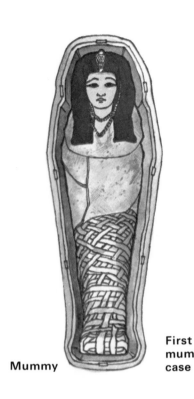

Mummy

First
mummy
case

Second
mummy
case

Mummies

The Egyptians tried to preserve dead bodies for ever by mummifying them. They cut out the soft parts of the body and put them in special jars. Then they washed out the inside of the

Making
mummies

body and filled it with spices. Finally, they wrapped it up in sticky bandages from head to foot. Sometimes the gum on these bandages caused the body to rot instead of preserving it.

When the mummy was ready, it was placed in a coffin or mummy case. This coffin was placed in another larger coffin. A picture of the dead person was painted or carved on the outside.

The golden coffins of the pharaohs were carried in ships to the pyramids

Two Pharaohs

Rameses II

Rameses II is one of Egypt's best known pharaohs. He lived from 1290 BC to 1224 BC. Rameses loved fighting. He fought the fierce Hittites who lived in present-day Turkey. A famous battle was fought at Kadesh in modern Syria. Rameses led the Egyptian army. After a long battle, the Hittites withdrew. Rameses claimed a great victory.

A statue of Rameses II being built

Later, Rameses made peace with the Hittites and married their King's daughter. He marched deep into Africa and conquered lands there. He also fought with the Minoans of Crete. Rameses expanded and ruled the Egyptian empire for forty years.

When the Aswan Dam was built, huge statues of Rameses and his wife at Abu Simbel were in danger of being covered by water

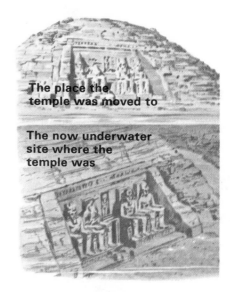

The place the temple was moved to

The now underwater site where the temple was

The huge statues were cut into blocks and moved to a spot higher up on the cliffs

Akhenaton

Nefertiti

Akhenaton

In 1375 BC a very unusual man became king of Egypt. His name was Amenhotep IV. He did not believe in the old gods. He believed only in the sun god, Aton, and changed his name to Akhenaton. He left Thebes, the old capital of Egypt, and built a marvellous new capital at Amarna.

Akhenaton was married to a beautiful woman called Nefertiti. They had six daughters. Akhenaton did not believe pharaohs should live like gods, so he and his family lived ordinary lives.

Akhenaton did not like the stiff old styles of art. He liked carvings and paintings to look like real people. When sculptors carved statues of him, he insisted that they showed his pot belly.

In 1369 BC, Akhenaton died. Tutankhamen, the new pharaoh, was only twelve years old and listened to the advice of Nefertiti. Then, three years later, Nefertiti died. When he was about eighteen, Tutankhamen died. Some historians think he was poisoned.

Tutankhamen's Tomb

One of the treasure rooms in
Tutankhamen's tomb

In 1922, an English archaeologist, Lord Carnarvon, and his
friend Howard Carter were digging in the Valley of the Kings.
In fact, they had been digging there for six years without
finding anything exciting. Then, on 4 November 1922, they
found the entrance to King Tutankhamen's tomb.

When the workmen uncovered the doorway and cleared the
entrance passage of stones, they found a second door.
Carnarvon and Carter were excited. Had tomb robbers been
there before them? Carter made a little hole in the second door
and peeped in. 'Can you see anything?' asked Lord Carnarvon.
'Yes', replied Carter. 'I can see wonders.'

Inside the tomb

When the door was opened, they discovered a room full of treasures. There were statues, a beautiful throne, some furniture, vases and many other things. Then, they found another room full of riches where everything was tipped upside down. Perhaps the guards had surprised robbers in the tomb and fought with them.

Finally, they found another door. What lay beyond it? When they opened the door, they saw the yellow gleam of gold. They found themselves standing in front of a beautiful golden shrine. Carter opened its doors only to find another shrine inside. In fact there were four shrines one inside the other. At last they came to a great yellow stone coffin.

The lid of the coffin was so heavy that it had to be lifted off by a machine. Inside there was a beautiful golden coffin, with a little bunch of dried flowers lying on it. Who had put them there? Perhaps, it was Tutankhamen's sad young wife several thousand years ago.

There were three coffins in all. When they had all been opened, Carter could see the mummy of the dead king. The bandages were cut away. Tutankhamen looked calm and almost happy as he lay there.

One of the golden coffins covering Tutankhamen's body

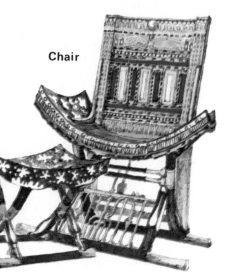

Chair

Drinking cup

Some things found in Tutankhamen's tomb

Necklace

Folding stool

Writing and Measuring

The papyrus plant

First layer

Second layer

Sticking the
strips together

Polishing
the paper

Making papyrus paper

Papyrus

Papyrus plants grow in thick clumps in the marshes along the River Nile. The Egyptians found many uses for papyrus. They made baskets and ropes with it and sucked it like sugar cane. But paper was the most important thing made of papyrus. In fact, our word paper comes from the Egyptian word papyrus.

Making paper

To make paper, papyrus plants were peeled and cut into flat strips. The strips were laid side by side. More strips were laid on top of them in the opposite direction. The strips were crushed under weights. Sticky juices held them together. The papyrus was dried in the sun. Finally, the paper was rubbed and polished.

Scribes

Scribes kept the official records in ancient Egypt. They were among the few people who could read and write. The scribes kept their ink on a board called a palette and wrote with a reed pen called a stylus.

The Egyptian word meaning 'to write'. It is made up of the signs for palette, papyrus and scroll

A scribe at work

Hieroglyphics

The Egyptians had several different ways of writing. The most famous one is called hieroglyphics, which means priest carvings. The priests carved hieroglyphics on temples.

Hieroglyphics were a form of picture writing. At first, each sign was a picture of a real thing. Later signs were put together to make more difficult words. When the signs for palette, papyrus and scroll were put together, they made the word 'to write'.

Hieroglyphics were painted or carved on stone

Finding the Rosetta Stone

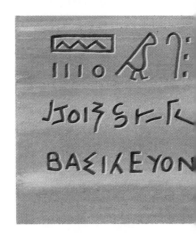

The Rosetta stone

The Rosetta Stone

For a long time historians could not read hieroglyphics. In 1799 some French soldiers discovered an important stone tablet at a place called Rosetta in Egypt. On it, a royal order was written in three different scripts. They were hieroglyphics, demotic which was a kind of hieroglyphic 'shorthand' and Greek.

Many scholars could read Greek. A Frenchman, Jean Champollion, studied the stone. He noticed that all the pharaohs' names were surrounded by a frame called a cartouche. By comparing the names in hieroglyphics with those in Greek, he was able to discover how to read hieroglyphics.

The three scripts. At the top, hieroglyphics. In the middle, demotic. At the bottom, Greek

70

An Egyptian sundial

An Egyptian sundial

Time and calendars

The Egyptians were very good at measuring time. At night, they used the stars. During the day they used sundials. The shadow cast by the sundial told them what hour of the day it was.

Egyptian priests studied the sun and the stars and worked out an accurate calendar. It had 365 days in a year. The priests used the calendar to tell the people when the River Nile would flood.

A water clock. Pots like this were used to measure how much time had passed

An Egyptian calendar

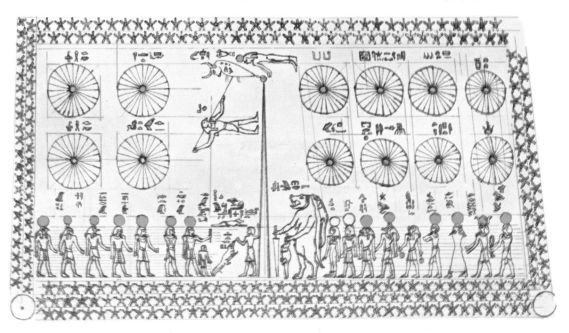

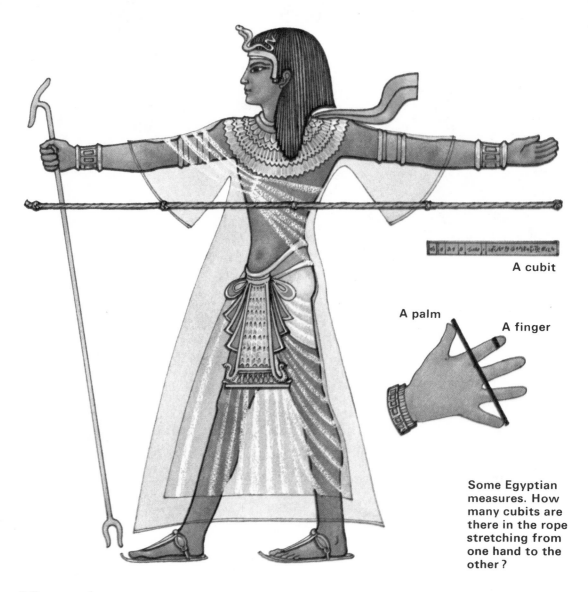

A cubit

A palm

A finger

Some Egyptian measures. How many cubits are there in the rope stretching from one hand to the other?

Measuring

The Egyptians measured things in fingers, palms, cubits and atons. A finger was the width of a finger. A palm was the distance between the thumb and little finger when the hand was open. A cubit was the distance from the elbow to the fingertips.

There were four fingers in a palm, and seven palms in a cubit. An aton was made up of twenty thousand cubits.

Try measuring a table in palms and fingers. What did you get? Ask a few friends to measure the same table. If they get a different answer, it is because everyone's hands are not the same size. The Egyptians solved this problem by fixing a standard measure.

The standard measure for a cubit was often carved on the temple wall. Everyone could compare his arm with the standard cubit.

Grains and other goods were measured in tubs of a set size. A common measure for liquids was the hon.

Numbers

The Egyptians were first-class mathematicians. They had different signs for ones, tens, hundreds, and thousands.

The Egyptians knew how to measure an area in square cubits and atons. They could work out angles, especially right angles. The Egyptians used these skills for practical purposes. They needed them to measure the size of fields and to build great buildings such as the pyramids.

This man is measuring his arm against the standard cubit carved on a temple wall

Two Egyptian measures

Working with numbers

Egyptian numbers

| 1 | 2 | 3 | 4 | 5 | 6 | 7 | 8 | 9 | 10 | 100 | 1000 |

What is this number?

73

Houses, Clothes and Furniture

Making sun-dried bricks

Houses

Egyptian houses were made of sun-dried bricks and had hardly any windows. Poor people lived in simple houses with one or two rooms. The roofs were flat. People liked to climb up onto the roof at night and sleep there in the cool.

The houses of rich people were built around courtyards. There were usually water tanks and small gardens in the courtyards. Inside, there were many rooms.

The home of a poor family

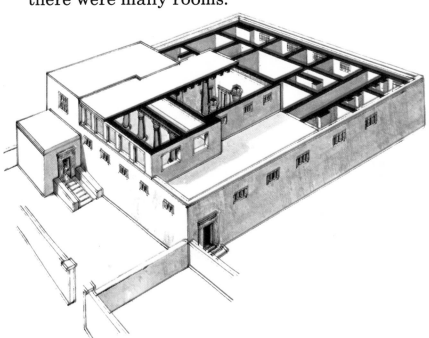

The home of a rich family

74

Clothes

Clothing was very simple in this hot country. The women wore light linen dresses made from flax. Ordinary men wore loincloths held up by belts. Rich men wore pleated kilts and flowing robes. Boys often went around naked and girls wore white tunics.

The women wore make-up. Men and women wore wigs. Sometimes they put a knob of sweet smelling fat on their foreheads. When they perspired, it melted and ran down their faces giving off a pleasant smell.

An Egyptian mother and baby

Furniture

The Egyptians did not have very much furniture compared with ourselves. However, a rich family would have had a number of chairs, tables, beds, and clothes' chests. This furniture was beautifully painted. It was often inlaid with pieces of ivory, a blue stone called lapis lazuli and a red stone called cornelian.

A rich family would have had chairs and tables like these. They would have slept on beds like the one on the right

Ships and Traders

A ship made of bundles of reeds

The first Egyptian ships were made of bundles of papyrus reeds.
The reeds were turned up at the ends. The ships were steered
by large paddles. They had one large mast and a square sail.
They were blown along by the wind or rowed along with oars.

Later, the Egyptians made wooden ships. These ships had
gaily painted deck-houses where the passengers and crew could
escape from the heat of the Sun.

Egyptian ships sailed across the Mediterranean Sea to Crete.
Here the Egyptians bought olive oil and wine from the Minoans.
They also sailed through the Red Sea to East Africa. They
brought back a hard black wood called ebony,
ivory and ostrich feathers.

Egyptian ships sailed far and
wide in the Mediterranean
and Red Seas

Women wove their
cloth on horizontal
looms

Things to trade

The Egyptians made many
beautiful things. Some of these
were sold to other countries.
Many people prized the thin
cloth the Egyptians made from
flax. Egyptian jewellery was
also traded. Some of the gold
used to make jewellery came
from East Africa. Precious
stones were brought from East
Africa and the Far East.

Gold workers made
beautiful jewellery.
Ornaments like this
scarab beetle were
made of gold and
precious stones

Egyptian potters made fine
pots. Sometimes these were
sold with goods inside.
Small stone cosmetic jars were
filled with perfume or
eye-colouring and sold abroad.

Potters used a
wheel to make fine
pots

Craftsmen made
life-like clay
animals like this
hippopotamus

Soldiers and Warfare

For many years the pharaohs did not keep large armies or try to conquer other lands. The Egyptians were no match for the better trained armies of neighbouring kingdoms.

Around 1600 BC, the Egyptians changed their way of fighting. They began to fight with horses and chariots as their enemies did.

Some chariots held only one warrior who tied the reins to his belt to free his hands for fighting. Others carried a driver and a soldier who fired arrows at the enemy.

Several kinds of foot soldiers followed behind the chariots. Archers carried axes and clubs as well as bows and arrows. Spearmen carried two metre long spears and huge shields.

Many foreigners fought in the Egyptian army. Some were paid and given special privileges. Others were prisoners of war. Between 1600 BC and 1150 BC the Egyptian army conquered a large empire. Eventually, they were defeated. The great days of Egypt were over.

The city of Mohenjo-daro probably looked like this

THE INDUS VALLEY PEOPLE

In the centre of Mohenjo-daro was a large sunken bath

Archaeologists have been working for years to solve the mystery of the Indus Valley cities. The two greatest cities were Harappa and Mohenjo-daro. Both had wide straight streets with drains running alongside them. The buildings were made of bricks. The most important ones were built on high mounds overlooking the cities. The rulers probably lived here. Both cities have huge granaries where barley and wheat were stored.

Questions without answers

What is the great mystery about the Indus Valley? The cities were built around 2500 BC. So far, no one knows where the people came from or how the cities began. Usually, when archaeologists dig beneath a city, they can trace its slow stage by stage growth from a small village. This is not so in the Indus Valley. The cities seem to spring up out of nowhere.

The Indus people have left a few written records. But so far, no one has been able to read them. No one is sure how the cities were ruled or what gods the people worshipped.

There are many questions left to answer about the Indus people. Archaeologists have found a lot of clues. With these, we can build up a picture of how things might have been.

Archaeologists found modern-looking lavatories in many homes

Drains ran along the streets. They were covered with bricks

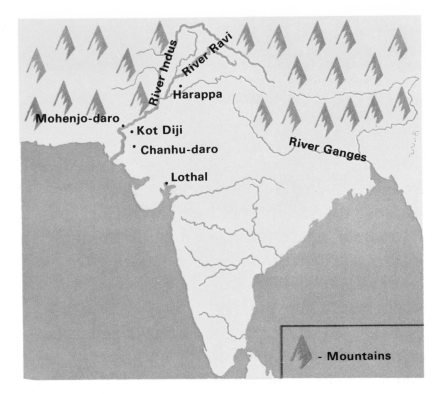

The map shows some of the main cities of the Indus Valley civilization. Can you find Harappa and Mohenjo-daro?

The Indus people grew melons, sesame, dates, wheat and barley

The Indus Cities

The granaries

Archaeologists are very interested in the huge buildings used to store grain in both Harappa and Mohenjo-daro. These were built on high platforms. The rivers probably flooded often. It was wise to keep the grain where the flood waters would not spoil it.

The granaries were made of bricks and wood. Special vents were made in the buildings to let in air to keep the grain dry.

The granary at Mohenjo-daro. Wheat and barley were brought from the fields and stored in the granary

At the Mohenjo-daro granary, there is a place where farmers could back up their carts to unload. Wheat and barley were probably brought from fields that stretched around the city.

Why did farmers bring their grain into the cities? No one is sure. Some people think that the Indus Valley was a harsh place to live. People may have worked together and saved the grain when they had a good harvest. That way there would be food during floods or when the crops failed.

The grain may have been taxes or gifts to the gods. Possibly the cities were ruled by strong kings or priests who wanted to control all the grain. That way they could be sure that people obeyed them.

An Indus merchant fixing his seal onto a package of goods

One big empire?

Over sixty Indian cities have been found that were built around the same time as Harappa and Mohenjo-daro. Most of the cities had straight wide streets. The weights and measures used were the same and people wrote the same way. Even the bricks used in building were usually the same size. No one knows if all the cities were ruled by one king.

The port at Lothal probably looked like this

A trading centre

Archaeologists have found one city that seems to have been a busy port. It is called Lothal. One of the warehouses along the dock probably burnt down thousands of years ago. In the ruins, archaeologists found many pieces of clay which merchants had stamped with their stone seals. They think merchants put a bit of wet clay over the ropes tied around bundles of goods. Then they stamped their seal on top of the clay.

Who did the people of Lothal trade with? They sent goods up to Harappa and Mohenjo-daro and much farther away. Stone seals from India have been found in Sumerian cities. The Sumerians wrote about a land called Melukka which was reached by a long sea journey. That land might have been India.

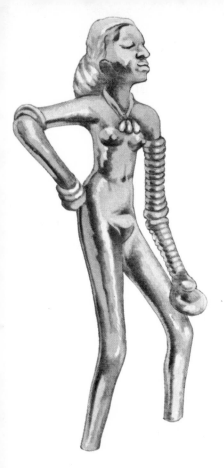

The dancing girl

Arts and Crafts

There are no huge statues of gods or kings in the Indus cities. Possibly the people made grand statues out of wood which have rotted away. Some small statues of metal and stone have remained to show what fine artists they were.

The statue of a man on the opposite page is less than half a metre high. His narrow eyes and stern look have made some people think he was a proud king. Others think he looks like a yogi or holy man in a deep trance. What do you think?

One of the finest statues is of a young girl. She is usually called the dancing girl. She is thin and naked except for a necklace and a mass of bangles that nearly covers one arm.

Jewellery

Women wore lots of jewellery. Rich women had necklaces, bracelets, earrings and rings of gold. They had many strings of stone beads. These were made of jade, agate, onyx and other stones. Some were carved in the shape of tiny monkeys and squirrels.

Men may have worn jewellery, too. The priest or king in the statue is wearing what seems to be a gold disc on a band around his forehead.

Indus jewellery

King or priest? ▶

86

Toys

Indus craftsmen also made interesting toys. There were clay whistles shaped like birds and small clay monkeys that slid down strings. Carts had moveable wheels so that they could be drawn from one place to another. Some clay cows were made so that when you pulled a string, the head bobbed up and down.

Many dice have been found which may have been used in games played by children and adults. Small clay figures may have been the pieces for a game like chess.

A boy blowing a whistle and a girl playing with a clay animal

A seal with writing

UY☐||Y☼

←

E⚹U||∞

The Indus script was written from right to left

Seals with mysterious words

The stone seals used in the Indus Valley show some of the artists' finest work. Many have beautiful life-like animals carved on them.

At the top of almost every seal, there is a name or message written in the Indus language. So far, no one has been able to read the signs.

We do know that the language was written from right to left because letters on the left often overlap those on the right.

Over two thousand seals with writing have been found. A group of archaeologists in Denmark has put all of this writing into a computer. They are hoping the computer will find the key to the Indus language.

Some seals had carvings of mythical beasts such as this three-headed animal

A rhinoceros seal and a rhinoceros

Indus animals

Although we cannot read the language on the seals, the pictures give us a lot of information. Many of them show the animals that lived in the Indus Valley.

From the seals, we know that long-nosed crocodiles swam in the rivers. Rhinoceroses with knobbly armour wallowed on the banks nearby. Elephants and tigers lived in the forests.

Many seals show bulls. These may have played a part in the Indus religion.

Not all of the animals on the seals are real. Some are strange beasts with three heads. These may have been gods or spirits.

A tiger seal and a tiger

A crocodile seal and a crocodile

Mysterious Gods

Archaeologists are still trying to put together a picture of the Indus Valley religion. Several seals show a goddess with horns lurking in the branches of a tree. She may be a tree spirit that people left gifts for.

Clay statues of a Mother Goddess have been found. She probably watched over women and children.

Several seals show a figure sitting cross-legged like a yogi or holy man. The modern god, Shiva, is often pictured the same way. He may be a god the Indus people worshipped thousands of years ago.

The Mother Goddess

Flowers left for a tree spirit

A god on an Indus seal

The modern god Shiva

90

The Fall of the Indus Cities

In about 1500 BC invaders attacked and destroyed Mohenjo-daro, Harappa and many other Indus towns. At Mohenjo-daro, archaeologists have found the skeletons of people who were cut down by the raiders. In one room alone, they found the bodies of thirteen grown-ups and a child. Two of the skulls had deep sword cuts in them.

Who were the invaders who attacked the Indus people? They were probably the Aryans who settled in India. It seems the Aryans only finished off the Indus cities. Before the last attack the cities were already dying.

What had happened? It may be that the Indus people cut down all the trees along the river to use in building and baking bricks. This would have made the floods worse. The floods may have ruined the soil. No one knows for sure. The fall of the Indus cities is one more mystery that is waiting to be solved.

These bronze pots were made over three thousand years ago. The people who made them were called the Shang

THE PEOPLE OF ANCIENT CHINA

A monster mask. Can you find it on the pot above?

A dragon from a Shang pot

The Shang people of ancient China were famous long before archaeologists found their cities. Stories of the great Shang kings had been passed down through the ages. Many of the beautiful bronze pots made by the Shang had been sold to museums. Some came from grave robbers and others from farmers who found them buried in their fields.

The Shang are still known mainly for these pots. They were used for special ceremonies and were so well made that even modern craftsmen could not better them. The pots were decorated with lines that made swirls and scrolls. Often the lines come together to make a face. The face is called t'ao-tieh, the monster mask. Sometimes the lines formed a dragon which curled its way around the pot.

The earliest Chinese

The Shang were not the first people to live in Ancient China. Over 600,000 years ago, early Stone Age men and women were living in the caves of Chou K'ou Tien near Peking. Over six thousand years ago the first farmers were growing wheat and millet and tending their pigs and sheep. It seems a second group of farmers moved into China from South-East Asia. They grew rice instead of wheat and millet.

When were the first Chinese cities built? No one is sure. The Chinese tell of a great line of kings who lived before the Shang. They are called the Hsia. So far, archaeologists have found no trace of them.

The first cities that have been found are those of the Shang. They were built around 1500 BC. The Shang capital, Anyang, was discovered in 1927. Archaeologists have been working at Anyang almost continually from 1927 to the present day.

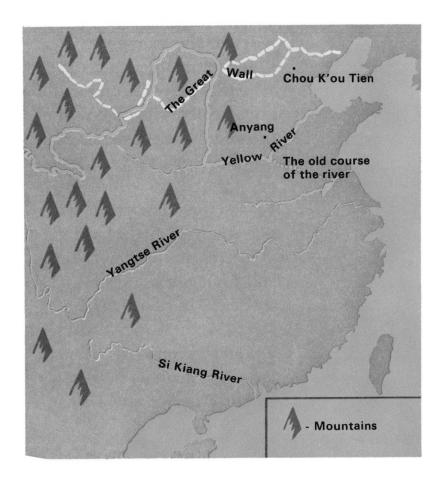

The main Shang city was called Anyang. Can you find it on the map?

The Burial of a King

The archaeologists digging at Anyang were lucky. It was not long before they found the graves of the kings. According to old stories, there had been twelve kings who ruled from the capital of Anyang. The twelfth had died in the blazing palace when the Shang were defeated by a neighbouring kingdom. Archaeologists found eleven royal graves – just the number one would have expected.

Gifts in the graves

When a king died, a great pit was dug in the ground and the king's coffin was placed in the middle. It seems the Shang people believed that their king had to take everything he needed for the next life with him when he died.

Grave robbers had taken many but not all of the treasures buried with the kings. Archaeologists found weapons, bronze pots, and jewellery made of gold, jade and bronze.

A bronze axe from a royal grave

Daggers made of jade found in a grave

Tiny jade animals from a grave

A Shang king is lowered into his tomb ▶

94

Sacrifices

The king's pet dogs were often killed and buried with him. His horses were also killed and buried still harnessed to their chariots.

People were also buried with the king. Who were they? Some of them seem to have been his favourite wives and friends. Others were probably slaves or prisoners taken in raids on enemy settlements. Some of the people were buried in coffins. Others had been beheaded. Their bodies and heads were buried separately. In one royal grave over a hundred human skeletons were found.

No one knows why so many people were killed and buried with the king. Some of them were probably meant to accompany the king in his next life. In later times, the Chinese people believed that the spirit of a dead king could bring them good or harm. They built shrines to their dead kings and sacrificed pigs and sheep to please the king's spirit. Possibly the Shang sacrificed people to please their dead kings.

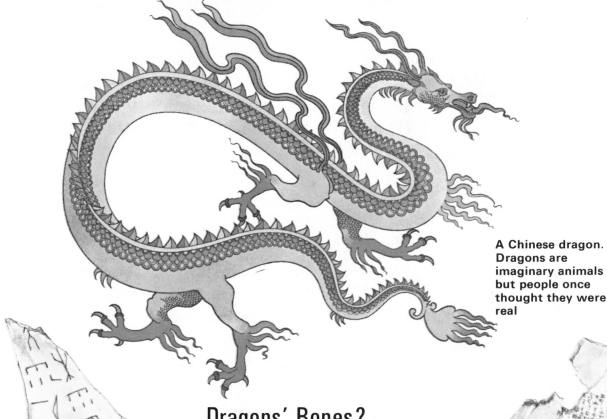

A Chinese dragon. Dragons are imaginary animals but people once thought they were real

The writing on oracle bones is like modern Chinese

Questions were written on oracle bones

Dragons' Bones?

For hundreds of years Chinese traders sold what they called dragons' bones. These bones were ground into powder and made into medicines. They were really the shoulder blades of oxen, sheep and pigs. In the ruins of Anyang, archaeologists found over ten thousand such bones.

Many of the bones had writing on them. It was the writing of the Shang people. The Shang had invented several thousand picture words. Modern Chinese writing can be traced back to the picture words of the Shang.

The Shang word for tree

The modern Chinese word for tree

Shang word for goat

The modern Chinese word for goat

Asking the oracle

What were the bones used for? They were oracle bones. Oracles are people or things that foretell the future. The Shang believed that the gods would answer the questions that they wrote on the bones. Small pits were made in a bone opposite each question. Then a red hot bronze needle was placed in each of the pits. The heat made the bone split. The cracks either meant 'yes' or 'no' to the question. On special occasions, the shell of a tortoise was used instead of a bone.

The Shang people made many decisions in this way. Their kings would not go to war without the support of the oracles. The ordinary people asked when to plough their fields and harvest their crops.

The Shang made decisions after consulting oracle bones

Li

Tsun

Chinese pots

Life in Shang Times

City life

The Shang built several cities. In the cities
the rich and powerful lived in great houses.
These were sometimes thirty metres long.
Their high pitched roofs were probably
thatched. The building was supported by rows
of wooden pillars.

Chariots raced through the city streets. They
had spoked wheels and were drawn by two or
four horses. In Shang times, the horses had to
pull the chariots with neck bands. These tended
to strangle them if they tried to go too fast.
Later, the Chinese invented chest bands so that
horses could pull chariots quickly without
choking.

A small house in the country. The floor is lower than the ground outside

Rich city dwellers used pots made of fine pottery and bronze. There were several different shapes. Pots called li stood on three small legs. Tsun were fine cone-shaped jars.

Ordinary people wore coarse cloth made of hemp, but rich people wore beautiful silk clothes. The Shang had learned how to spin and weave silk from the cocoons of silkworms.

A crowded city street in Shang times

Country life

In the countryside, people lived in round huts, much as they had during the New Stone Age. They were supported by wooden pillars and had a fireplace in the middle.

Farmers dug the fields with spades and digging sticks. The plough was not invented until after Shang times. With the plough, far more land could be farmed and much more food grown. The Shang farmers grew millet and barley in their fields and reaped their crops with stone sickles.

Life in Han Times

Building the Great Wall of China

In ancient times, China was ruled by a number of different royal families. All of the kings from one family are called a dynasty. The Shang kings were conquered by a neighbouring kingdom. The new kings formed the Chou dynasty.

Next came the Chin dynasty. The name China comes from the Chin. The Chin began to build the Great Wall of China to keep out tribes that were raiding the land. The Great Wall was restored by later kings. It still stretches across northern China.

Jade rings were buried with the dead

The jade burial suit of Prince Lin Shang who lived in Han times

One of the greatest dynasties to rule China was the Han dynasty. The Han kings ruled for over four hundred years from 206 BC to 220 AD. We know a lot about the lives of rich people in Han times from the things found in their tombs.

The Han people made clay models of houses, farms, pet animals and musicians and buried them with their dead. Their graves also contained jewellery, hair pins, mirrors, dishes and trays. Many tombs had carvings or paintings on the walls. Some of these showed officials travelling in horse-drawn chariots.

In one grave archaeologists found a prince and princess buried in jade suits. One suit was made of over two thousand pieces of jade sewn together with gold threads.

A pottery model of a Han house

Rich nobles rode about in horse drawn chariots with umbrellas or shades to keep off the hot sun or rain

101

Government officials

Ruling the land

The Han emperors were called the Sons of Heaven and their word was law. They ruled China through officials who were scattered throughout the land. These officials were chosen by public examinations. Young men came from all over the country to compete for positions.

Ancestor worship

In Han times, people believed that the spirits of their dead ancestors and kings could influence their lives. They built shrines and made offerings to please their ancestors and the spirits of their kings.

Confucius

Many people followed the teachings of Kung Fu-Tse or Confucius. Confucius lived from about 550 BC to 480 BC. His ideas did not become popular until after his death. He taught that people should try hard to be fair, kind, truthful, loyal and unselfish.

A modern statue of Confucius

Lao Tse

The teachings of Lao Tse were also popular in Han times. The followers of Lao Tse were known as Taoists. They believed people should live simple lives close to nature. They felt that finding inner peace was more important than improving society.

A modern statue of Lao Tse

The Yin and Yang

The Han also believed in the power of natural forces such as fire and water. They thought the world was ruled by two opposite forces called the Yin and the Yang. The picture on the right was used to represent these forces. The symbol in the middle stands for the mixture of the Yin and Yang in the world.

The yellow lines and the symbol in the middle stand for the yin and yang

In the villages

Farmers had a difficult life when the Han took over China. They had been taxed so heavily that many of them ran away from their farms. Han Kao Tsu, the first Han emperor, ended most of these taxes and gave the farmers a chance to recover.

The Yellow River had always been a great threat to farmers. When it flooded, its waters washed away villages, ruined crops and killed many people. The Han tried to stop the flooding of the Yellow River. The banks were strengthened and many canals were dug linking it to other rivers.

A farmer

Life on a farm

104

Silk weaving

Silk has been made in China since Shang times. During the
Han dynasty, better ways of spinning and weaving were used.
Beautiful patterns were woven in the silk, which was even finer
than before. Orchards of mulberry trees were planted to provide
leaves to feed the silkworms.

Acrobats

Entertainment

Rich officials and merchants
had many kinds of
entertainment. Some kept
their own musicians and
dancers so they could enjoy
a show whenever they wanted.
Groups of jugglers and
acrobats performed on special
occasions. They did hand-
springs and somersaults to the
music of bells hung from a
wooden frame and struck with
a hammer.

105

The famous 'flying horse'

Art

The Han artists were the first Chinese to make realistic looking animals and people. The bronze 'flying horse' shows how well the artist could represent animals. They were equally successful with people, as the figures below show.

The pottery figures are playing a game. It looks as though the man on the right has made a clever move

Paper making

The Han were the first people to make writing paper as we know it. At first they made it out of silk and hemp, but later they used tree bark and rags. Paper was far better to write on than the strips of bamboo they had used before.

Making paper

Writing on paper with a brush

Writing

The Han wrote with brushes rather than the pointed styluses used earlier. They made ink from pine soot mixed with glue and water. They also produced the first Chinese dictionary. It listed nine thousand words.

Camel trains on the Silk Road

Trade

The Han were great traders. Their goods went as far as Rome. The land route between Rome and China was called the Silk Road because the Chinese brought so much silk along it. The Chinese traders exchanged silk, furs and spices for glass, jade, horses, jewels and silver.

THE MINOANS

The Minotaur and the maze

The Story of Theseus

According to the Ancient Greeks, Crete was once ruled by a king called Minos. This king had a Minotaur for a son. The Minotaur was half man and half bull. This monster lived in a maze or labyrinth. King Minos forced Greek rulers to send young men and women to Crete to be sacrificed to the Minotaur.

Theseus and Ariadne

Theseus and Ariadne

One year, Theseus, the son of the King of Athens, went to Crete with some other young people. Ariadne, the daughter of King Minos, fell in love with Theseus. When it was Theseus' turn to be fed to the Minotaur, she gave him a sword and a ball of thread. Theseus tied the end of the thread to a pillar and walked bravely into the labyrinth.

108

Theseus meets the Minotaur

As Theseus went deeper into the maze, the roars of the monster became louder and louder. Suddenly, the Minotaur leapt out in front of him. Theseus pulled out his sword. After a terrible battle, he killed the Minotaur and followed the thread back to where he had left Ariadne.

Then, Theseus, Ariadne and all his Athenian friends escaped in Theseus' ship.

Is there any truth in this story? Until 1900, historians did not think so. But in that year an archaeologist called Arthur Evans started digging into a low hill just outside Heraklion in Crete. Almost immediately he uncovered the ruins of an immense wall and a store full of huge jars. These ruins were part of the once mighty palace of Knossos.

It may well be that Greek slaves were taken to Knossos and sacrificed to the Minoan gods.

The Island Kingdom

The first Minoans crossed the sea to Crete in about 8000 BC. They grew wheat and barley and raised pigs and sheep.

New ideas may have come to Crete with later settlers. Slowly the people of Crete built up the first European civilization.

A Cretan trading ship

A trading centre

By 2000 BC, Crete was a rich trading centre with fine cities and palaces. The Minoans traded with the Egyptians, the Mesopotamians and many other people. They became a powerful kingdom. People living on the mainland and on other islands nearby recognized the Minoans as their rulers.

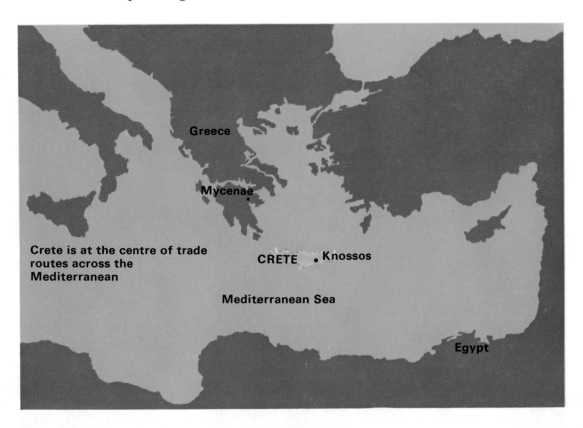

Greece

Mycenae

Crete is at the centre of trade routes across the Mediterranean

CRETE • Knossos

Mediterranean Sea

Egypt

People and Houses

Minoan men

The Minoans were short, dark-haired people. The men shaved off their beards with bronze razors, but let their curly black hair grow long. Their only clothing was a skimpy loin-cloth. They prided themselves on their tiny waists and pulled their belts as tight as possible.

The men wore leather sandals or went barefoot. They liked necklaces, armlets and anklets made of gold and silver.

Minoan men

Armour

Minoan warriors wore helmets with long plumes. They carried large shields shaped like rectangles or like figures-of-eight. The shields covered them from head to foot. They carried short daggers and long swords.

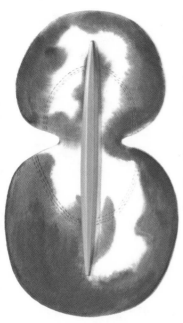

A figure-of-eight shield

A dagger and a sword

A helmet

111

Minoan women

Minoan women

Minoan women had long wavy hair that fell down on their shoulders in ringlets. They wore long bell-shaped skirts and little jackets.

Their make-up was kept in beautifully carved cases. They mixed blue and green tints for their eyes and reds for their lips on small stone palettes.

The goldsmiths of Crete made beautiful jewellery. The ladies of the court wore pendants shaped like birds and animals. Gold earrings dangled from their ears and delicate gold flowers decorated their hair.

A pendant shaped like two wasps

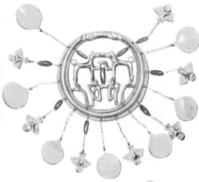

A piece of jewellery, probably an earring

Ivory jar for make-up

Tweezers

Stone palette

Hairpin

Things women used for their make-up and hair

Gold flowers

A gold pendant

112

Houses

The Minoans lived in well planned towns with paved streets. Their two or three storeyed houses were built of bricks or wood and plaster. They had flat roofs. Many houses had between six and eight rooms. The walls were often painted red and decorated with brightly coloured pictures.

The Minoans made these small models of their houses

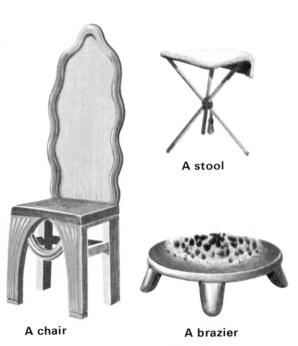

A stool

A chair

A brazier

Furniture

Minoan furniture was beautifully made. There were stone-topped tables, high-backed chairs and folding stools with cushions. People kept their clothes in wooden or clay chests. When people died, these chests were often used as coffins.

The houses were lit by clay lamps full of olive oil. In winter the houses were heated by braziers. These were stone or metal containers full of burning wood that could be moved from room to room.

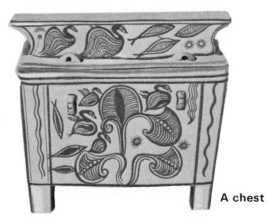

A chest

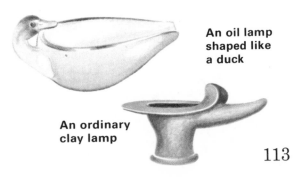

An oil lamp shaped like a duck

An ordinary clay lamp

113

Storage jars found
at Knossos

The palace of Knossos

The finest Minoan homes were the palaces where nobles lived. The most beautiful palace was at Knossos. It was built around a huge courtyard. Its broad open halls were lined with pillars. The buildings were several storeys high.

Light wells were built into the flat roofs so sunshine could stream into the rooms below. These were covered over in winter to keep the draughts out.

On the western side of the courtyard, there were lines of storehouses containing enormous jars. These were probably filled with olive oil and wine. There was also a fine throne room with a holy shrine. The walls were painted with rows of griffins. Griffins were imaginary creatures with birds' heads and lions' bodies.

A covered walk in
the palace at
Knossos

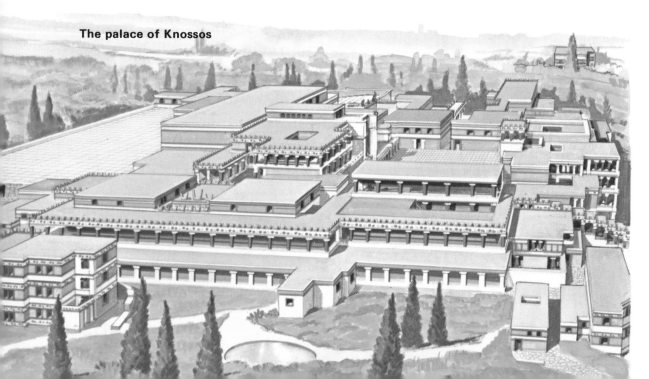

The palace of Knossos

The royal rooms

The living quarters were entered by a superb staircase. The first room was the Hall of the Double Axes. Here the king and his nobles relaxed. Huge figure-of-eight shields were painted on the walls.

The queen's room was further down the corridor. The walls were painted with lifelike dolphins and starfish. Next door was a bathroom decorated with spirals.

One of the best things about the palace was its plumbing. Clay pipes brought water to the palace from wells outside. Carefully planned drains took waste water and sewage away. The palace even had flush toilets.

Dolphins and fish painted on the wall in the queen's room

The queen's bathroom

An acrobat somersaults over a bull

Bull Leaping

The Minoans crowded together to watch one of the most amazing sports in the world's history. Huge, fat, slow moving bulls lumbered about an arena charging at groups of young, nearly naked men and women. These acrobats ran up to the bull, seized its horns and somersaulted over its back. It seems the acrobats worked in groups. Some acted as catchers and others as jumpers. If a jumper fell, he might die a terrible death.

A Minoan wall painting showing bull jumping

A bronze bull's head

The sacred bulls

What was the point of this sport? Bull jumping seems to have been part of the Minoans' religion. Bulls were sacred animals. Many beautiful statues of bulls and bull horns have been found in Crete. The Minoans may have linked the rumblings of earthquakes which often shook Crete with a great bull deep within the Earth. Perhaps the Minoans were trying to please this bull god.

Double axes used in religious services

The Mother Goddess

The Minoans also worshipped a Mother Goddess. They believed that she was the source of life. Every house had a shrine to her. The palace at Knossos had a great three-legged altar carrying bulls' horns and double axes. Animals were sacrificed here and their blood offered to the Mother Goddess.

The Minoans may have carried out their most sacred services in caves deep underground. Here priestesses dressed like the Mother Goddess danced and prayed.

A statue of a goddess

117

Reading Minoan Writing

When Arthur Evans was digging amongst the ruins of Knossos, he found many clay tablets and seal stones. Both were covered in picture writing rather like Egyptian hieroglyphics. Here, Evans thought he had found a valuable source of information about the Minoans.

For years Evans studied these tablets. After a time he decided that they were written in two different styles. He called one Linear A and the other Linear B. He also discovered that the Minoans had written from left to right as we do, but this was all he did discover. Both languages remained a mystery.

Linear A

Linear B

The Minoan script

In the 1930's Arthur Evans gave a talk on Minoan Crete to an audience in London. One of the listeners was a thirteen year old boy called Michael Ventris. He decided to make the study of these tablets his hobby. Many years later, Ventris managed to match up some fifty Linear B signs with Greek letters.

Since then, not much progress has been made. Some people think that Ventris' readings may be wrong. Even if they are right, the Minoan tablets still hold many secrets.

118

The palace at Knossos may have been destroyed by an earthquake

The Fall of the Minoans

The marvellous Minoan towns and palaces were destroyed in about 1400 BC. What happened? Historians hold two views. The first is that Crete was attacked by fierce invaders. The second is that the cities were destroyed by earthquakes. Arthur Evans held this view. He felt that warriors would have needed bulldozers to knock down the cities so completely!

Both explanations may be right. It is possible that a great earthquake destroyed the cities and that the Minoans' enemies took advantage of the situation and invaded the island.

Evans found scorch marks on the walls near oil jars. This seems to show that the palace burnt down

119

The Lion Gate of Mycenae. The arrow shows where it stood at the entrance of the city.

The People of Mycenae

If Crete was invaded by enemies, they probably came from Mycenae in Greece. These fierce warriors lived in a great fortress built on top of solid rock. The fortress was surrounded by gigantic walls. Over the top of the main gate two lions were carved out of stone.

The Mycenaeans loved fighting. They wore leather armour and leather helmets decorated with boars' tusks. They carried shields and cut their enemies down with sharp bronze swords.

The Mycenaeans were great sailors and traders like the Minoans. With the fall of Crete, their power became even greater.

A helmet covered with boars' tusks

A dagger found in the grave of a Mycenaean warrior

The graves of Mycenae

In 1876, an archaeologist called Heinrich Schliemann found the graves of several Mycenaean warriors. Gold death masks covered their faces. Spears, daggers and shields were buried with them.

A gold death mask which had been placed over the face of a Mycenaean warrior

One of the daggers shows hunters attacking a lion. One man is using a bow and arrow while others are throwing spears.

The archaeologists found nine other graves cut out of the sides of the hills. The finest is called the Treasury of Atreus. It has a grand gateway. The roof of the burial chambers forms a great dome.

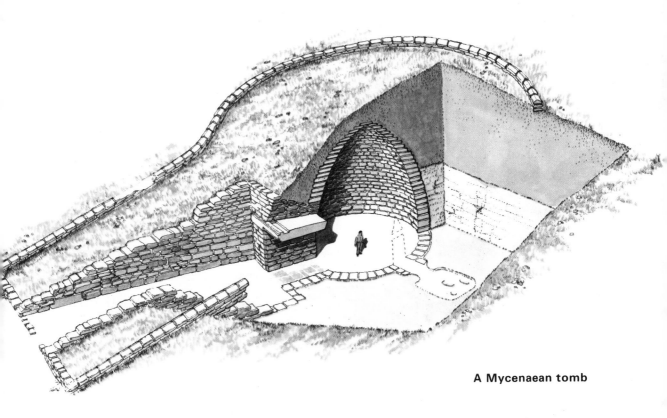

A Mycenaean tomb

The Parthenon, one of the most beautiful buildings in the world

THE GREEKS

Athenian men and women often walked along the hilly paths leading to the acropolis. They stopped to visit the Parthenon, the main temple of the goddess Athena.

The Greeks were great builders and the Parthenon was one of their most beautiful buildings. Tall graceful pillars lined the front. Above the pillars were stone carvings by the great sculptor Pheidias.

A gold and ivory statue of Athena stood inside.

Greek cities

Beautiful buildings such as the Parthenon were only one of the achievements of the Greeks. Between 900 BC and 400 BC, they enjoyed one of the finest civilizations in the world's history. At the centre of Greek life was the city or polis.

A Greek home

Greece is a hilly country so most of the cities were built close to the seashore. In most cities, the main buildings were built on a hill called the acropolis. Acropolis means upper city. The acropolis served as a fortress in times of danger.

The houses of the ordinary people crowded around the acropolis. These houses were built around an open courtyard. The walls were made of thin plaster. They were so flimsy that burglars dug holes right through them. The Greek word for a burglar means wall-digger.

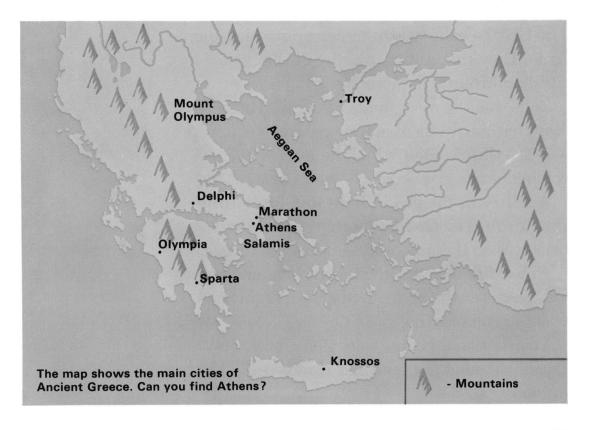

Mount Olympus

.Troy

Aegean Sea

.Delphi

.Marathon
.Athens
Salamis

Olympia.

.Sparta

.Knossos

The map shows the main cities of Ancient Greece. Can you find Athens?

- Mountains

Gods and goddesses

The Greeks believed that gods controlled their lives. They thought that many of the gods lived on Mount Olympus.

Zeus was the most important god. His wife was Hera, goddess of marriage. His weapon was the thunderbolt which he hurled at wrongdoers.

Apollo was the god of light and foretelling the future. The Greeks thought that his priestess at Delphi could see into the future.

Aphrodite was the goddess of love and beauty and Demeter the goddess of crops. Dionysus was the god of wine.

Poseidon and Hades were Zeus' brothers. Poseidon ruled the seas and Hades the underworld.

The god Pan had a man's body and a goat's legs and tail. He was the god of flocks and herds. Each Greek town chose one god or goddess as their special protector. The Spartans worshipped Artemis, the goddess of hunting, while the Athenians favoured Athena, the goddess of wisdom and peace.

The Greeks also believed in many lesser gods like the Naiads and Dryads. The Naiads were the spirits of the streams and rivers while the Dryads were the spirits of the trees.

Gods and goddesses. From left to right Apollo, Aphrodite, Demeter, Dionysus, Zeus, Poseidon and Hades

Pan, the god of flocks and herds

125

Athens

The City-States

Greece was divided into many separate city-states. Each was made up of one main city which controlled the land around it. The city-states had their own governments and armies.

Athens was one of the most powerful city-states. It was a democracy where every citizen had the right to take part in the government. Athenians were proud of the great artists, poets and playwrights who lived in their city.

Sparta was a powerful city-state quite different from Athens. The Spartans lived a hard life with few luxuries. Boys were sent to be trained as soldiers when they were seven years old. Sparta had fine warriors, but few artists or playwrights.

Sparta

Building the Parthenon

Beautiful Buildings

The Greeks had three different styles of building. They are called Doric, Ionic, and Corinthian. It is easy to tell them apart by the pillars used for each. The top of a pillar is called the capital. Doric columns were short and plain with a simple, cushion-like capital. Ionic columns were thinner and had a fancy capital with curves which looked like rams' horns. Corinthian columns were the thinnest. Their capitals were decorated with leaves.

The Greeks built important buildings of marble. They did not have cement to hold the blocks together. Instead they used iron rods and clamps.

The three Greek styles of pillars

Doric   Ionic   Corinthian

127

Phoenician	Greek		Latin
𐤀	Α	Alpha	A
𐤁	Β	Beta	B
𐤂	Λ	Gamma	C, G
𐤃	Δ	Delta	D
𐤄	Ε	Epsilon	E
𐤊	Κ	Kappa	K
𐤋	L	Lambda	L
𐤌	Μ	Mu	M
𐤍	Ν	Nu	N
𐤐	Γ	Pi	P
𐤓	Ρ	Rho	R
𐤅	Σ	Sigma	S

Homer

Stories and Plays

Why do we write the way we do? We got our alphabet from the Romans. The Romans took theirs from the Greeks and the Greeks borrowed theirs from the Phoenicians who lived near present-day Syria.

The Greeks wrote laws, geography, history, plays and poetry.

Two famous poems of the Greeks are the Iliad and the Odyssey. They are said to have been written by a wandering story-teller called Homer. The Iliad is an exciting story about a Trojan prince, Paris, who carried away the Greek queen, Helen.

Paris and Helen

Helen was the most beautiful woman in the world and the Greeks joined together to get her back. After ten years of war with the Trojans, the Greeks finally thought of a cunning scheme.

The Trojan horse

They built a large wooden horse and hid Greek soldiers inside. Then they sailed away. The Trojans thought that they had won. They pulled the horse inside the city and began to celebrate. The Greeks inside the horse slipped out and opened the city gates for the Greek army which had returned. The Greeks stormed into Troy. They won the war and carried Helen back.

The Trojans pulling the Greek horse into the city

Watching plays

The Greeks loved watching plays. Every year during the holidays in honour of the god Dionysus, they went at sunrise to watch as many as four plays a day. Anyone who was too poor to pay for a ticket could get one free from the city officials. The plays they saw were either tragedies which ended sadly, or comedies which made people laugh.

The theatres

Greek theatres were large and in the open. They were often built on the side of a hill. The seats stretched in a semicircle around the stage.

Thousands of people could see a play at one time. In the centre of the stage was an altar. Behind it was a small building where the actors changed into their costumes.

Actors' masks

An open-air theatre

Greek actors. Women were not allowed to act in plays so men took the women's parts

The actors

Greek actors wore masks to show how they felt. Some masks were smiling and some gloomy. The masks contained small megaphones so the actors' voices would carry farther. The actors wore raised shoes, wigs and padded clothes so the audience could see them better. A group of people called the chorus spoke from time to time. They explained the story to the audience.

The play

Most plays were based on well known stories, so there were few surprise endings. People were curious to see how a playwright told an old story. Prizes were given every year for the best plays. Among the most famous playwrights were Aeschylus, Sophocles and Euripides.

Sophocles, one of the most famous Greek playwrights

131

At a Greek Market

A bustling Greek market

Many Greeks farmed the fields which stretched around each town. They grew wheat and barley and had grape vines and olive trees. They kept sheep and goats but few cattle, because there was not enough hay to feed them in the winter.

132

Buying and selling

Soon after sunrise, the country people went to the local town to sell their vegetables, fruit and wine. The market was called the agora. It was divided up into streets where everybody sold the same things. There were streets of bread-sellers, wine-sellers and fruit-sellers.

Greek men did much of the shopping. They loved to bargain. The seller of the goods always asked for too much money and the buyer always offered too little. Then they argued about it until they both agreed on a price.

There were streets full of craftsmen such as carpenters, potters and metal workers. People could stop and watch them at work as their workshops were open to the street.

Some of the finest craftsmen were potters. They turned their pots on a potter's wheel to make beautiful shapes. Some pots were painted with a special mixture before they were baked. The plain clay turned red in the oven while the painted parts turned black.

Farmers collecting olives. This picture is copied from a Greek vase

Two different kinds of drinking cups

A jug for storing and cooling wine

A decorated jug used to mix wine with water before serving it

School scenes from a Greek vase. On the left a boy is playing a lyre and on the right a boy is having a reading lesson with his teacher

Boys writing on wax tablets

Schools and Sports

Boys were sent to school when they were about seven. Slaves usually went along to carry their books and keep an eye on them. The boys studied Homer's 'Iliad' and 'Odyssey'. They learnt much of them by heart.

They wrote on waxed tablets using a pointed pen and worked out sums. Most Greeks liked mathematics so much that they drew problems in the dust and worked them out as a game.

Before starting the games, boys rubbed their bodies with olive oil

Sports were an important part of every boy's education. Each day the boys went to the sports arena and did exercises to the sound of flute music. As soon as they had loosened their muscles they ran and jumped, threw the discus or javelin, and boxed or wrestled.

Afterwards they scraped all the dirt and sweat from their bodies with a tool called a strigil. Then they had showers or baths.

Crowning a winner

A hockey player

A javelin thrower

The Olympic games

Games were held at Olympia in Greece every four years in honour of Zeus. Men and boys came from all over Greece to take part in the running, jumping, boxing, wrestling and horse and chariot racing.

The winners of the events were regarded as heroes. Their home towns often built statues in their honour. The highest honour of all was to win the two hundred metres race. The winner was crowned with a circle of olive leaves.

Wrestlers

A discus thrower

135

Hairstyles worn by
Greek women

The chiton could be worn in two different
ways. The Dorian chiton is shown on the
left and the Ionian chiton on the right

A servant brings a women her jewellery

Greek women and children

Life at Home

The home in ancient Greece
was mainly a woman's world.
Most men had an early
breakfast and then went out
for the day. They came back
for dinner late in the evening.

The women looked after the
children and made sure that
meals were cooked and that
the house was kept clean and
neat. They did not have to do
all of the work themselves.
They had slaves to help them.

Women's clothes

The women wore a
comfortable kind of dress
called a chiton. It was slipped
over the head and tied at the
waist. They also wore
beautiful gold jewellery. They
let their hair grow long and
fixed it in many different ways.

136

Learning at home

Girls did not go to school. Their mothers taught them to cook, sew and keep the house in order. Some girls were taught to read and write by an educated slave. They learned to play the lyre and sing.

Women playing stringed instruments. This picture is taken from a Greek vase

Weaving

All of the cloth that a Greek family needed was woven at home. The Greeks told the story of a woman called Arachne. She boasted about her fine weaving and challenged the goddess Athena to a contest. When Athena won, Arachne hanged herself. Athena took pity on her and turned her into a spider so that she could weave beautiful webs.

Spinning and weaving took up a lot of time

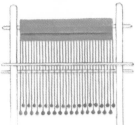

The pictures below tell the story of the contest held between Arachne and Athena

137

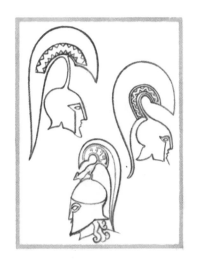

A hoplite or foot soldier

Soldiers and Sailors

Most Greek city-states had good armies. All young men had to train as soldiers for at least two years. In times of war, all healthy men fought in the army.

The Greek foot soldier was called a hoplite. He wore a helmet with nose and cheek pieces. He protected his body with a breastplate and his legs with bronze guards called greaves.

He carried a huge round shield that covered his body from chin to knee. His weapons were a three metre long spear and a short iron sword.

The hoplites fought shoulder to shoulder. A regiment or phalanx was usually made up of eight long lines of soldiers. The phalanx charged at a quick march because the soldiers' armour was too heavy to allow them to run.

On flat land the Greeks were more than a match for anybody. They proved this by defeating a huge army of Persians at the battle of Marathon in 494 BC.

Several kinds of helmets worn by hoplites

Nine years after the Battle of Marathon, the Persians attacked at a place called Salamis. For some time it looked as though the Persians might win. The Greeks finally defeated them in a sea battle

A Greek warship

Warships

The Greeks were also marvellous sailors. They built wooden warships called triremes. These ships were rowed by over a hundred oarsmen. They had a mast and a big square sail. The sail was lowered during battles.

The prow or front end of the trireme ended in a sharp point called a ram. The Greeks sailed straight at enemy ships and tore great holes in their sides.

▲ A Greek warrior ran 224 kilometres from Marathon to Sparta to ask the Spartans for help against the Persians. After the battle he ran from Marathon to Athens to announce the victory. At the Olympic Games, the Marathon race is held in his honour

Ships for trading

Not all Greek ships were warships. Some were built for trading. These were rounder and stronger so that they could be filled with goods. They had one large sail and no oarsmen. They made their way slowly from one trading port to another.

The Greek merchants carried wine and olive oil to ports around the Mediterranean Sea

Greek ships were loaded with wine, olive oil, and pottery to sell. Greece was too hilly and rocky for wheat to grow well. Traders brought back bags of wheat, timber and slaves.

Sailing a trading ship was often risky. Storms blew up and tossed the ships against the rocky coast. Pirates lay in wait to steal their goods. Many ships ended up at the bottom of the sea.

Divers have found the wrecks of merchant ships. Some of the wine jars were still intact

Greeks abroad

Many people moved away from Greece to start new settlements. They made new homes in places around the Mediterranean Sea where they could find land to farm. Trading ships brought wheat, timber, iron and copper from these settlements to Greece. They took the settlers the things they needed from the homeland.

Greek coins of Alexander's time

A mosaic picture of Alexander the Great. Mosaics are made of small pieces of stone and glass

Alexander the Great

In 356 BC, the greatest conqueror in the world's history was born in the small Greek state called Macedonia. His name was Alexander. His father was King Philip of Macedonia.

Alexander was taught by the famous Greek thinker, Aristotle. When he was still young, he showed his bravery by taming a wild horse called Bucephalus.

When Alexander was only twenty years old, his father was murdered. Alexander became King of Macedonia. He soon convinced all the Greek city-states to make him their leader.

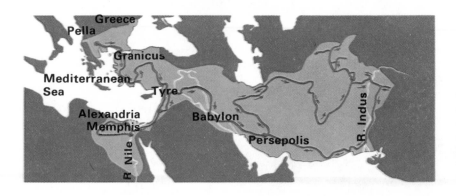

The blue line on the map shows the route Alexander took. The light brown area shows the lands he conquered

Alexander's victories

Alexander formed a great army. He asked the priestess at Delphi if he could defeat the Persians. She said that he could not be beaten. Alexander defeated the Persians. Then he conquered Palestine, Syria and Egypt. The Egyptians made him their pharaoh.

Although his soldiers were tired, Alexander led them over the mountains into India. They fought a big battle against an Indian king called

A battle scene on a Greek vase

Porus. The Indians used war elephants. Alexander worked out a plan to scare the big animals. When the elephants got close to the Greek army, the soldiers beat their swords against their shields and shouted. The elephants were terrified and ran back, trampling the Indian troops. Alexander won.

The Greek soldiers had now had enough so Alexander turned back. Near Babylon, Alexander fell ill and died. He was only thirty-two years old.

Alexander leading his troops

143

THE ROMANS

The founding of Rome

The Romans believed that Rome had been founded by a king called Romulus. According to the story, Romulus and his twin brother Remus were left in the River Tiber in a cradle when they were babies. When the cradle was washed ashore, the hungry babies were looked after by a she-wolf who fed them. Later a shepherd found them and brought them up as his own sons.

When the twins grew up, they built a city on the place where they had been found. The brothers quarrelled and Remus was killed. Romulus became the first king of Rome.

The spread of Roman rule

Rome began as a small city-state. The Romans built it into a great empire. They had to fight many battles to win new lands.

Some kings joined their lands to the Empire without fighting. The Roman Empire included all the lands around the Mediterranean Sea.

Romulus and Remus being fed by the she-wolf

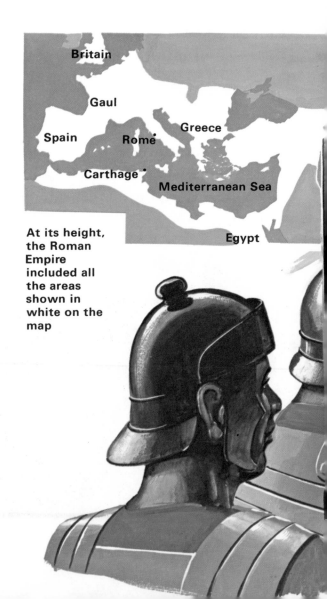

At its height, the Roman Empire included all the areas shown in white on the map

144

The Roman Army

Though the early Romans fought hard, they did not have a full-time army. Many of them owned small farms. After fighting a war, they would come home to plough their fields or harvest their crops. As Rome conquered more and more lands, soldiers had to stay far away from home for longer periods of time. Finally, the Romans set up a full-time permanent army. Romans joined the army for a fixed period, usually twenty years. When they retired, they were usually given a small plot of land to farm.

The Romans set up a full-time army. The soldiers were well trained and the army well organised

A foot soldier

Dividing up the army

The Roman army was divided into regiments called legions. Each legion had about five thousand men. They were grouped into ten cohorts of about five hundred men each. A cohort was made up of six centuries with eighty to a hundred men in each.

Each legion had its own standard with a golden eagle at the top. Under it were plaques to mark the battles in which the legion had fought well.

A soldier from the cavalry

Weapons and battles

Roman soldiers wore breastplates made of metal and leather helmets. They fought with short swords and javelins. Early Roman soldiers carried oval shields. Later, they had huge rectangular shields.

The Romans planned each battle carefully. The cavalry played an important part. Usually the foot soldiers marched straight at the enemy, while the cavalry attacked them from the sides.

When the legionaries attacked a wall, they covered their heads and bodies with their shields. They looked like a giant tortoise

When the legions attacked the walls of enemy towns, they raised their shields and locked them together. This formation was called a testudo, which means a turtle. The Romans used huge catapults to hurl stones or giant arrows at the walls.

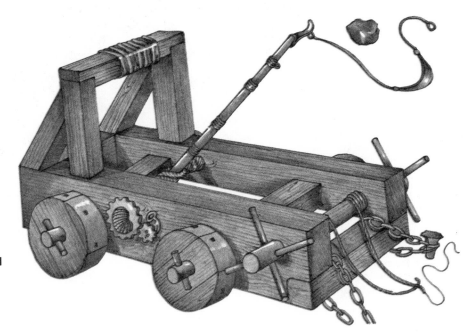

Catapults were used to knock holes in the walls of enemy cities

A Roman galley. The spiked bridge was
dropped onto an enemy ship so that the
Roman soldiers could run across and
capture it

Roman ships

Roman warships were called galleys. Some had over a hundred oarsmen. Each ship had a ram at the end of its prow, like Greek warships. The Roman galleys rammed enemy ships. Then the soldiers lowered a bridge. A spike at the end of the bridge stuck into the enemy ship. The soldiers ran across the bridge and fought with swords.

A Roman merchant ship

Many pirates roamed the Mediterranean Sea robbing trading ships. The Roman navy spent much of its time searching for pirates. It was so successful that the Mediterranean Sea became safe for traders for the first time for many years.

The Romans were great traders themselves. Merchant ships sailed to lands around the Mediterranean and beyond. Many goods were brought overland to sea ports, where Roman traders bought them. The traders brought spices from India and silk and perfumes from China to Rome.

Roman warships were rowed by slaves. There were three banks of oars. The oarsmen probably sat like this

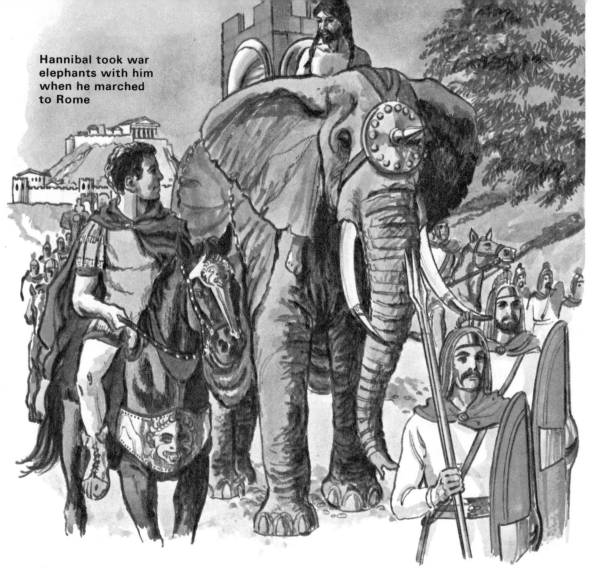

Hannibal took war elephants with him when he marched to Rome

Rome's greatest enemy

Have you ever heard the story of the general Hannibal? He led an army with elephants across the mountains called the Alps.

Hannibal came from Carthage, a powerful country which stretched from northern Africa into Spain. The people of Carthage were Rome's greatest enemy.

Hannibal's army crossed the Alps successfully and defeated the Romans in many battles. Hannibal marched his army right up to the walls of Rome, but could not fight his way in.

In 207 BC, the Romans gathered new armies. They trapped Hannibal's brother, Hasdrubal, in northern Italy.

He was bringing more troops and supplies to Hannibal. The Romans killed Hasdrubal and threw his head into Hannibal's camp.

150

The fall of Carthage

The Romans had a great general called Scipio. He led the Roman army to northern Africa to attack Carthage. Hannibal returned home to defend Carthage. In 202 BC Scipio's army won. It was Hannibal's first and last defeat.

The Romans tore down the walls of Carthage. The lands ruled by Carthage became part of the Roman Empire.

The red arrow shows Hannibal's route. He defeated the Romans in two great battles at Lake Trasimeno and Cannae

Hannibal's death

Hannibal fled but the Romans sent men after him. For many years he wandered from place to place. Then in 183 BC the Romans caught up with him and surrounded the house where he was staying. Hannibal killed himself rather than be captured.

Crossing the Alps

Roads Leading to Rome

The Romans built roads connecting all parts of
their huge empire. Their roads were built so
well that many of them can still be seen today.
The roads were made of layer after layer of
material. At the bottom there was usually a
layer of sand. Next came layers of flat stones,
pebbles, and gravel. The surface was covered
with stone slabs. The roads sloped away from
the centre so that rain water drained off the
sides.

Most roads were built by Roman soldiers
with the help of local people. A milestone was
placed beside the road at the end of every mile
so travellers knew how far they had gone.
Every twelve miles there was a post house
where the traveller could spend the night.

The Romans built
roads wherever they
went. They made
them as straight as
possible so that
soldiers could
march quickly from
one place to
another

A Roman milestone

Have you every heard the saying 'all roads lead to Rome'? Rome was the centre of the empire, and the roads kept Rome in touch with its far-away lands. Messengers sped along the roads carrying orders from the Emperor. Soldiers marched at a steady pace. Traders travelled slowly in carts loaded down with goods.

Roman roads were usually straight. Skilled engineers travelled with the Roman army to direct the building of roads. Sometimes tunnels had to be cut through rocks or bridges built across swiftly flowing rivers.

The Appian Way was one of the most famous Roman roads. It is in almost as good a state today as it was in Roman times

Building a bridge. A heavy stone attached to a pulley was used to drive piles into the river bed

Ruling Rome

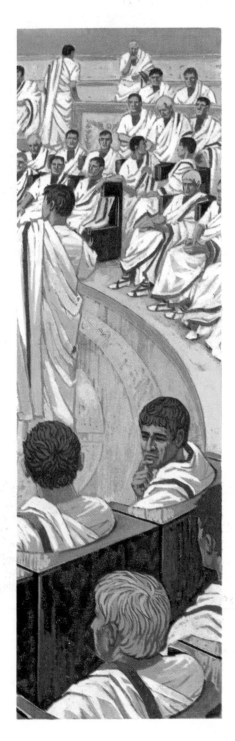

The Roman Senate

The Republic

In early times, the Romans were ruled by kings. But they soon drove out the kings and became a republic. The republic was ruled by a Senate which the people elected. There were six hundred senators.

The Senate chose two consuls each year. These consuls controlled the meetings of the Senate and led the Roman army in times of war.

The Empire

Some men began to think that it would be better to have one emperor who would make all the decisions. Julius Caesar was the first Roman to try and make himself emperor. He was murdered by a group of senators who thought that Rome should stay a republic.

However, Caesar's nephew became the first emperor of Rome in 27 BC. He was the Emperor Augustus. Augustus was one of the best emperors the Romans ever had. He ruled for forty years. The Romans named the eighth month of the year, August, after him.

From 27 BC until about 430 AD, Rome was ruled by emperors. Many, such as Hadrian and Marcus Aurelius, were sensible and hardworking. Some, such as Caligula and Nero, were cruel and selfish.

Two consuls led the Roman army and presided over the Senate

Two censors carried out a census to see how many Romans there were

Eight praetors were judges

Proconsuls and propraetors governed the provinces of the Roman Empire

A high priest organised official religious occasions

Twenty quaestors collected the taxes

Four aediles looked after the markets, the police and the public games

Officials of the Senate

During the Republic, many people helped to rule Rome. Some of them were officials of the Senate. The praetors were the judges and the quaestors were in charge of collecting taxes.

Ten tribunes looked after the rights of the poor

Paying taxes

Julius Caesar talking to a leader of the Gauls

The greatest Roman of all?

Julius Caesar was one of the greatest Roman generals and politicians. He was a good speaker and made the people of Rome feel that he was their friend.

Caesar wanted to lead an army of his own. He persuaded the Romans to send him to Gaul, modern France, with his own troops. His soldiers loved him because he was a brave and skilful leader.

Caesar conquered all of Gaul. In Rome, some people were afraid that he was becoming too powerful.

Caesar was captured by pirates when he was a young man. He captured them later and had them all hanged

Caesar went to Egypt and met Cleopatra. Later another Roman, Mark Antony, fell in love with Cleopatra

Caesar returns to Rome

The Senate ordered Caesar to disband his army and return to Rome alone. If he did not, they said, he would be declared an enemy of Rome. Caesar disobeyed them. He led his soldiers into Rome. Many of the senators fled.

Caesar became the most powerful person in the Empire. The Senate made him dictator for life. Many senators thought Caesar wanted to be king. On 15 March 44 BC, a group of them stabbed him to death in the Senate building.

Ceasar's death

A Day in Ancient Rome

What was it like to live in ancient Rome? This is how an imaginary Roman senator Marcus Livius Drusus spent a typical day.

The morning

Drusus got up at dawn, put on his toga and gave offerings to the household gods. Then he ate some bread and wine for breakfast.

Soon, the doors of the house were opened and visitors hurried in. Like most senators, Drusus was a lawyer. Many people came to ask him to handle their cases.

A Roman house. Houses were heated by hot air from a fire rising through spaces between the walls, floors and ceiling

The forum

At the forum

Drusus saw his visitors briefly. Then he set off
for the forum, the centre of Rome. The forum
was an open meeting place surrounded by law
courts, temples and other public buildings.

On the way to the forum, Drusus passed a
barber's shop where he could see young men
having their hair oiled and curled. There was
also a school. He could hear the howls of the
unhappy pupils who were being beaten!

On reaching the forum, Drusus entered the
Law Courts, and appeared before the Praetors
in several cases involving his clients. Then, he
made his way to the Senate. He listened to the
debates and made a speech.

A teacher and
student

159

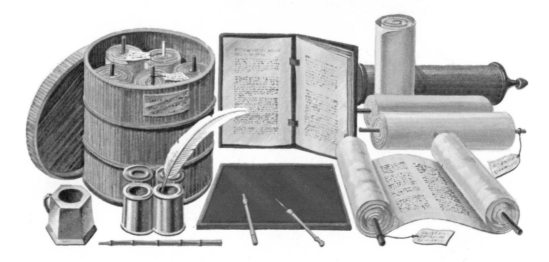

Roman books and writing materials

Home for lunch

At midday, Drusus' work was finished. He returned home for lunch. On the way, he stopped at the Sosii Brothers' shop to have a look at any books that had just come in. Books were copied by hand and were very expensive. Drusus had a room in his house set aside for his books. It was called the librarium.

Behind the bookshop, the slums began. Drusus rarely went there. Instead, he went through the market where slaves were being sold. When he arrived home, his lunch was waiting.

A slum

The slave market. Most slaves were captured in wars. Many of them were highly educated and looked after their master's businesses

At the public baths

The afternoon

After lunch, Drusus had a short sleep. Then he set out for the games fields. Like most Romans, he believed in keeping fit. He had a game of ball before making his way to the baths.

Most Romans visited the public baths every day. Drusus got undressed and went into the caldarium, the hot room. Here he sweltered in the steam until the pores of his skin were open. Then he scraped the dirt and sweat from his skin with a metal scraper. When he was clean, he went into a cooler room, the tepidarium. Finally he jumped into a cold pool in the frigidarium. Then he had a massage, put on a clean toga and returned home.

The evening

Drusus usually had several guests for dinner. Dinner was the biggest meal of the day. The guests arrived and lay down on couches. Slaves brought the food in and put it on low tables. There were spiced eggs and small salads to start with. Then came roast meats and stuffed birds. Finally they had fruit and cakes. While they drank wine, Drusus and his guests were entertained by dancers and acrobats.

A banquet

Then it was time for talk. Drusus liked this part of the evening best. The men talked about the plays written by the Greek playwrights. They argued about which was best. Then they discussed the government of Rome.

Soon Drusus' guests had to hurry off. They wanted to get home before dark because the streets of Rome were full of robbers. Then Drusus went to bed.

Temples and Gods

Many Roman gods were similar to Greek gods. Jupiter ruled the other gods. Juno was his queen. These gods were worshipped in large temples.

A household shrine

The Pantheon, a large Roman temple

Household gods

The Romans also had household shrines. Here they made offerings to the Lares and Penates, the gods of the home and cupboards. Every house also had an altar to Vesta, the goddess of fire.

The Christians

The Romans often worshipped the gods of the people they conquered. They also thought that their emperor was a god.

A small group of people said that there was only one God. These were the followers of Jesus Christ. They were called Christians. The Romans felt that the Christians were being disloyal because they would not burn incense to the emperor. They threw many Christians to the lions.

Many Christians were fed to the lions in the Circus Maximus

164

Great Buildings

The Romans were fine builders. They often used the arch. This was a semicircle of brick or stone resting on pillars. Arches were used in building roofs, windows and doorways.

The arch was seen at its best in the bridges and aqueducts built by the Romans. Aqueducts were huge bridges carrying water from high lands into towns.

Roman builders invented the dome. A dome is a high rounded roof. Domes were used mainly for big buildings.

Concrete was another Roman invention. They made it of sand and lime mixed with water. It was poured into wooden moulds. It hardened and became very strong.

The Romans used the round arch. The bricks were held up with a wooden frame until the mortar dried

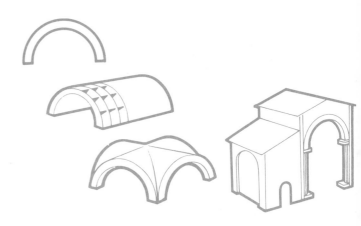

The arch was very useful in building. A series of arches could be used to make a vaulted roof

Aqueducts carried drinking water from the hills into Roman towns

Water

The Romans often carved elaborate capitals on top of columns. This one is made up of beautifully carved leaves

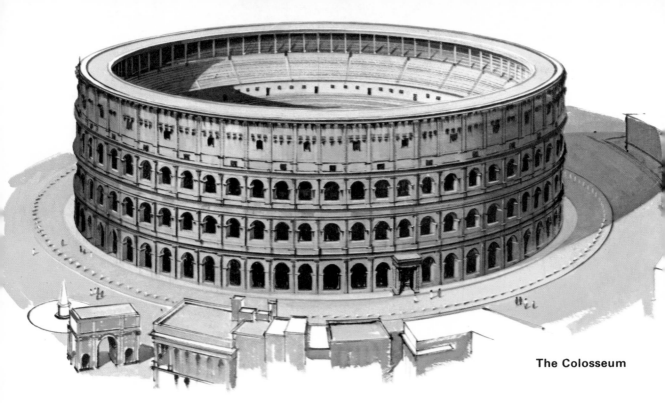

The Colosseum

Gladiators and Chariot Races

The Romans loved fighting. On public holidays, they went to huge arenas called amphitheatres.

The crowds went to see the gladiators fight. Usually two gladiators met in the centre of the arena. One carried a net in which he tried to entangle his enemy. He had a three-pronged fork called a trident. He tried to pin down the other gladiator with it. The second fighter wore a large helmet and carried a shield and sword. Usually the gladiators fought to the death.

Chariot races took place in the Circus Maximus. Many drivers and horses were killed

Gladiators fighting in an arena

Sometimes, a beaten gladiator was given his life by a happy crowd. If they wanted the fallen man to live, they waved their handkerchiefs. If they wanted him to die, they turned down their thumbs.

The Romans particularly enjoyed chariot racing. In Rome, these took place at the Circus Maximus. Huge crowds of nearly 400,000 people watched the chariots dashing round the sand covered track.

The volcano, Vesuvius, erupting

The Story of Pompeii

Pompeii was a Roman city built at the foot of Mount Vesuvius. In 79 AD, Vesuvius suddenly erupted. Glowing red hot lava poured down the side of the volcano. Smoke and ashes filled the air. The people of Pompeii rushed through the streets trying to escape.

Many people were overcome by the sulphur gas and died. Soon the town was covered in a thick layer of lava, mud and ashes. Pompeii remained buried for hundreds of years.

The nearby town of Herculaneum was also buried in lava. In one house, archaeologists found the body of a boy who was about to eat a meal. His legs may have been paralysed

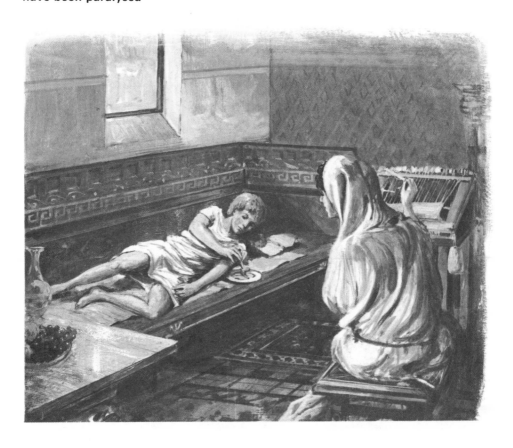

A rich family's house as it would have looked before the volcano erupted

Archaeologists have been working at Pompeii for many years. Today, visitors can walk down the empty streets and through the forum where the market was held. They can see the temples, law courts, and baths.

In Pompeii, the homes of the rich and poor were preserved just as people left them. Because of this terrible disaster, we know more about the daily life of the Romans than any other ancient people.

A room in Pompeii today

Archaeologists uncovering the Maya cities

THE MAYA

The Maya built their cities in the jungles of present day Mexico, Guatemala and Honduras. Huge pyramid-shaped buildings towered high above the green umbrella of jungle trees. The greatest Maya cities were built between 300 AD and 900 AD. Then, the cities were forgotten. The trees and vines of the jungle took over the land again.

It was not until the 18th century that the Maya cities were discovered by archaeologists. They had to hack their way through the dense jungles to get to the lost cities.

Archaeologists found many carved stones

170

The first Americans

The ancestors of the Maya and other American Indians probably came to America between twenty and thirty thousand years ago. They crossed the Bering Strait from Asia and spread throughout North, Central and South America. They settled down in different areas and formed different societies.

In about 5000 BC some of the Indians in Central America started to farm the land. Most archaeologists believe that the Indians made this discovery without help from the outside world. Several thousand years passed before the Maya built one of the earliest and greatest American civilizations.

NORTH AMERICA

Aztec

Maya

SOUTH AMERICA

Inca

The arrows show the route that people coming from Asia to America took. Many settled down and built villages and towns along the route

The map shows the areas where the Maya lived

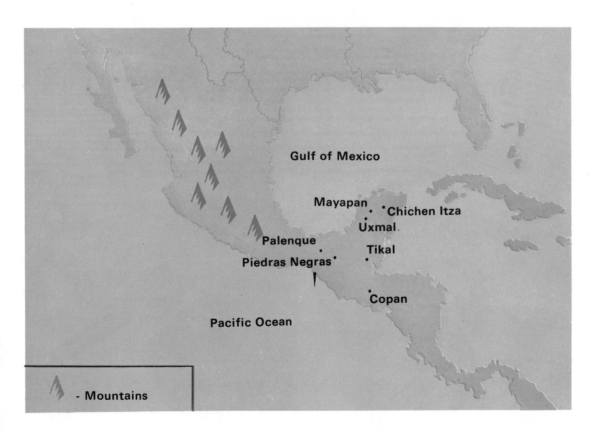

Gulf of Mexico

Mayapan
Chichen Itza
Uxmal
Palenque
Tikal
Piedras Negras

Copan

Pacific Ocean

- Mountains

171

Maya Cities

The Maya cities were not cities as we know them. They were used mainly for religious purposes. The kings and priests were probably the only people who lived in the cities and possibly even they did not do so. The ordinary people lived in villages some distance from the towns. They spent their time working in the fields or building the temples and palaces.

A Maya pyramid temple

Players on a ball court

The ball courts

All Maya towns were built on a similar plan. Every town had a special ball court where a game called pok-ta-pok was played. It seems the game was played with solid rubber balls. The players were only allowed to hit the ball with their shoulders, hips, knees and forearms. To score, a player had to knock the ball through a ring on the wall of the court. These ball courts are similar to those used in Central America in later times.

Playing pok-ta-pok. What modern game does this remind you of?

Building the temples

The main buildings in every Maya city were the great terraced pyramids built on raised platforms. Some of them were over sixty metres high with stairways leading to a small temple at the top. Here the priests burnt incense and performed secret ceremonies for the gods. The Maya had no metal tools. All of the work on these huge pyramids had to be done with stone tools. The Maya did not have donkeys, horses, oxen or any other beasts of burden. They made toys with wheels, but it seems they never used the wheel for transportation. All of the huge stones used to make their pyramids and palaces had to be moved and lifted by the muscles of the workers.

A Maya chief
making an
offering to the
sun god

Gods and Goddesses

The Maya had many gods. The supreme god
seems to have been Itzamna. It was said that he
invented writing. He was the god of learning
and heaven. His wife Ixchel was the goddess
of weaving, medicine and childbirth.
Among the many other gods, the one that
appears to have been the most important was
Yum Kax. He was the god of maize. Since the
Maya depended on maize for food, they paid
great attention to Yum Kax. Chac was the god
of rain. Ah Kinchil was the sun god.

Itzamna

Offerings for the gods

To keep the gods pleased, the Maya made many kinds of offerings at their temples. Usually they offered food, both cooked and raw. But on some big feast days, the Maya believed the gods needed blood. The Maya then offered both the blood of animals and their own. They sometimes cut a finger or some other part of their body to collect blood to offer to the gods. Sometimes, the priests felt a person should be offered to the gods. The person sacrificed was usually a prisoner or a slave. To please the rain god Chac, human victims were sometimes thrown into a well.

A Maya statue showing a man sticking thorns in his tongue and offering the drops of blood to a god

Ixchel

Yum Kax

The gods and the world

The Maya believed the world was flat. Each of the four corners had a special colour. Red was for the east, white for the north, black for the west, yellow for the south, and green for the centre. There were gods at the four corners who held up the sky.

Above the Earth there were thirteen layers of heaven, each with its own god.

175

Astronomy, Numbers and Writing

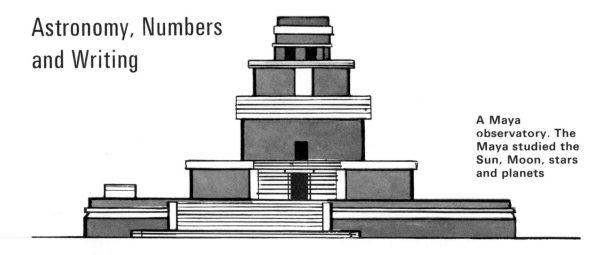

A Maya observatory. The Maya studied the Sun, Moon, stars and planets

Calendars

The Maya were very interested in time. They had two calendars. The tzolkin was the religious year of 260 days. Every day was named after one of the gods.

There was also an ordinary year of 365 days called the haab. The haab was made up of eighteen months of twenty days each plus five extra days. These were thought to be very unlucky.

Inside the observatory

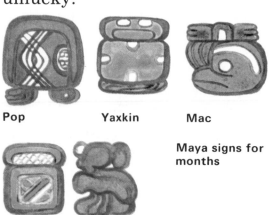

Pop Yaxkin Mac

Maya signs for months

Zio Muan

Studying the stars

Several Maya buildings were probably used as observatories. Here, the priests studied the movement of the stars and planets. We do not know what tools they used, but their measurements were very accurate. For example, they knew how long a year is on the planet Venus.

176

Working with numbers

The Maya were very good at mathematics. They were the only people apart from the people of India to have invented the zero. They wrote zero with a shell-shaped sign.

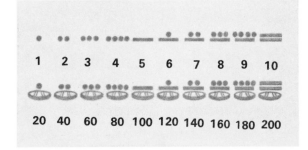

Maya numbers

Folding books

The Maya made paper out of long strips of bark. They pounded the bark into thin sheets and covered it with a layer of sticky gum and then with lime. Maya books folded out into one long sheet.

Only a few Maya books have survived to the present day. They seem to be stories about the gods and records of the stars and planets. The Maya wrote with picture-signs called hieroglyphics. Some Maya writing has been translated, but much is still a mystery.

Carving hieroglyphics

A page from a Maya book

A Maya folding book

The Rulers and the People

The Maya were ruled by their priests and nobles. The priests were teachers, doctors, engineers and fortune tellers. They were a hereditary class. In other words, fathers passed on their jobs to their sons. The boys received a long training. They had to be taught to read and write. They had to learn how to design the cities and how to foresee eclipses of the Moon and Sun.

The priest wore huge feather headdresses covered with jade ornaments. Their cloaks were made of bright feathers or jaguar skins.

Maya nobles

The temple pyramid at Palenque where the tomb of a high priest was found

The tomb of a priest
In 1952 a Mexican archaeologist found the tomb of a high priest hidden inside the pyramid at Palenque. The priest was buried in a magnificent stone coffin with a carving of a handsome young man on the lid. Underneath was the body of the high priest still dressed in jaguar skins and covered with jade jewels.

178

A village chief and his servants

The nobles

The Maya nobles were the heads of the villages.
They were in charge of everyday affairs. They
had to see that the ordinary people paid their
taxes of food and cloth.

They wore splendid clothes. As well as the
usual feather headdresses and loincloths,
they wore rings, necklaces and nose ornaments.
These were made out of jade, jaguars' claws,
alligators' teeth and gold.

The Maya had no chariots. When the nobles
went out, their servants carried them in
covered chairs.

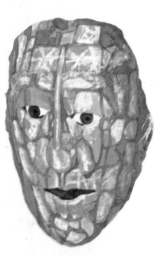

The death mask of
the high priest
buried at Palenque

179

Village life

The houses of the ordinary people were in the villages. The Maya made their homes of woven twigs covered with mud. Large forked tree branches were used as frames for the house. Most houses were raised on a small platform of dried earth and stones. This kept the rain water out. None of the houses had windows.

The ordinary Maya worked hard and long. They owned little but a few pots, some flint knives and a set of grinding stones.

A Maya village

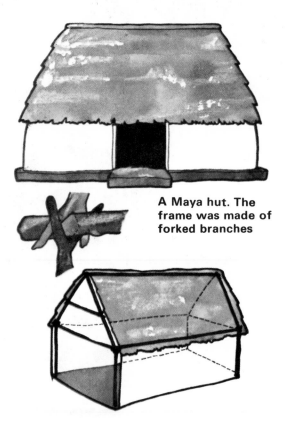

A Maya hut. The frame was made of forked branches

There were no schools for the children of ordinary people. The girls were taught by their mothers.

The boys were taught to farm by their fathers. The Maya used the same methods for thousands of years. They cleared their fields by cutting down a stretch of jungle and burning the trees. They farmed the same area until the soil was worn out. Then they cleared new lands.

The Maya never invented a plough so they had to turn over the soil with digging sticks.

The Maya grew crops of maize, beans, squashes, melons and sweet potatoes. They kept turkeys and small hairless dogs for food.

Wild deer, birds and other animals lived in the forests. The Maya hunted them with spears, bows and arrows and blow guns.

The Maya caught frogs, fish and tortoises in the lakes and rivers.

Although all these foods were eaten from time to time, the main food in Maya villages was maize. It was ground and eaten almost every day.

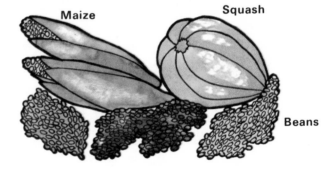

Maize

Squash

Beans

Crops grown by the Maya

A Maya hunter using a blow gun

Invaders and War

The temple of the god Kukulcan at Chichen Itza

Empty cities

In about 800 AD, the Maya left many of their southern cities. The tall buildings were quickly covered by a tangle of creepers and bushes. For a long time, archaeologists could not understand why the Maya left their cities. Then they noticed that the carvings in one city had been damaged. Looking more closely, they saw that the heads of all the statues of priests had been carefully cut off.

Statues like this one are called Chac-mools. The Itza probably left gifts for their gods on the plate on the figure's stomach

An uprising?

Archaeologists think that there may have been an uprising of the ordinary people against the priests. Perhaps the people grew tired of working their hearts out for cruel masters and decided to put an end to it. If there was an uprising, it only took place in the southern cities.

182

The Toltec invaders

Around the same time, the cities in the north were invaded by the Toltecs from central Mexico. The Maya called these fierce warriors the Itza. The Itza settled down to live among the Maya. Their chief god was Kukulcan. The Itza thought he wanted many human sacrifices.

A throne in the form of a snarling red jaguar. It was found in a temple at Chichen Itza

Statues of the Plumed Serpent, Kukulcan

The Itza forced the Maya to worship Kukulcan. Kukulcan means feathered serpent. In statues, he is shown as part bird and part snake. The Itza fought many wars to get prisoners to sacrifice to Kukulcan.

Chichen Itza was the capital of the Itza empire. It had many superb buildings. One of the finest is the temple of Kukulcan which stands on top of a twenty metre pyramid.

Jaguars eating human hearts were carved on Itza temples

183

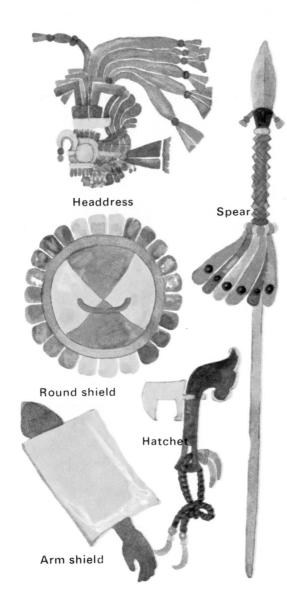

Headdress

Spear

Round shield

Hatchet

Arm shield

The weapons, shields and headdress of a warrior

From peace to war

In early times, the Maya were not great warriors. They lived peacefully and did not like to fight wars. When the Toltecs began to rule the Maya cities, life was no longer as peaceful.

Armies and weapons

The Toltecs needed captives to sacrifice to their gods. Soon the Maya cities were resounding to the sound of marching feet.

The soldiers used shields made of cotton, hardened deerskin or jaguar hides. They fought with bows and arrows and flint-tipped spears. They had no metal weapons. They used swords made of wood edged with razor sharp obsidian blades. They carried great stone hammers and clubs.

At a battle

The armies marched to the thunder of drums and the scream of conch shells. The warriors often painted their faces black, red and white. They carried bombs full of hornets to throw at the enemy. When the bombs burst among the enemy soldiers, the furious hornets stung everyone nearby.

At the end of the battle, the winners rounded up their prisoners and marched them off to their own cities. Some may have been made slaves. Others were taken to the temple and sacrificed to the gods.

Warriors driving prisoners before them

Human skulls stuck on poles are carved along a platform at Chichen Itza. The skulls of enemy warriors were probably displayed on top of this platform

Warriors travelling in canoes

Index

Acknowledgements

The author and publishers gratefully acknowledge the help given by the following in supplying photographs on the pages indicated:

British Museum 38, 92, 101, 106B
British Museum (Natural History) 20, 21
British Tourist Authority 31
French Tourist Authority 32
Sonia Halliday 142
William MacQuitty 65, 87, 105, 106T, Endpapers

The author and publishers also wish to thank the following artists whose illustrations are included in this book:

Fred Anderson/The Garden Studio, Marion Appleton, Sandra Archibald, Robin Arkle, Carol Barker, Peter Connolly, Esme Eve, Charmaine Fraser/ David Lewis Management, David Godfrey/ David Lewis Management, Donald Goff, Eric Jewell Associates, Tessa Jordan, Gordon King, Ken Kirkland/ Spectron Artists, Barbara Lake/Tudor Art Agency, P. McGinn/ John Martin and Artists, P. North/ The Garden Studio, Jennifer Parsons/Spectron Artists, K. J. Petts, Jeroo Roy/ Tudor Art Agency, E. Scott-Jones, John Smith, Ron Stenberg, Ross Wardle/Tudor Art Agency, Maurice Wilson

Grateful acknowledgement is made to Lorna Collins for her help in picture research and to Eileen Pears, Jennifer Moorby and Colin Trevorrow for their advice on vocabulary and subject matter suitable for the young reader.